Astrology

Make Better Decisions to Achieve Your Dreams

(A Guide to Understanding Your Birth Chart, Star Sign, and Ideal Relationship Partner)

Norris Sommers

Published By **Darby Connor**

Norris Sommers

All Rights Reserved

Astrology: Make Better Decisions to Achieve Your Dreams (A Guide to Understanding Your Birth Chart, Star Sign, and Ideal Relationship Partner)

ISBN 978-1-998927-36-4

No part of this guidebook shall be reproduced in any form without permission in writing from the publisher except in the case of brief quotations embodied in critical articles or reviews.

Legal & Disclaimer

The information contained in this book is not designed to replace or take the place of any form of medicine or professional medical advice. The information in this book has been provided for educational & entertainment purposes only.

The information contained in this book has been compiled from sources deemed reliable, and it is accurate to the best of the Author's knowledge; however, the Author cannot guarantee its accuracy and validity and cannot be held liable for any errors or omissions. Changes are periodically made to this book. You must consult your doctor or get professional medical advice before using any of the suggested remedies, techniques, or information in this book.

Table Of Contents

Chapter 1: Astrology – History of Astrology - Ancient and Modern Astrology

Modern Trends & History

The Mayans and Indians were the first to tell of ancient cultures that expressed their fascination for the astronomic bodies. Evidence from cave walls that show illustrations and markings that are attributed back to Babylonian society shows that our ancestors didn't just observe the celestial movements, but also studied them. These studies were later used by farmers and priests as well as kings.

Observation was a critical activity in these cultures, and those who are able to observe and interpret have been valued members these ancient societies.

It was so crucial to study these celestial body that those who discovered its meaning became powerful, influential people. These people ruled the ancient empires and kingdoms. They had their court fortune tellers, royal advisers, and imperial Astrologers.

As empires expanded across new continents so did astrology. It was soon adopted by European and Middle Eastern monarchies. Galileo Kepler Chaucer Chaucer, Chaucer, Shakespeare, as well as other philosophers and scientists of the early days, were both astrologers.

In fact, in those medieval days, there was no distinction made between astrology as a science or a practice. Astrology was studied and used alongside medicine and science, such as physics, meteorology and astronomy. Astrology was the basis of everything starting with a commoner's decision about marriage, a tradesman's choice of where to open a shop, and ending with a king declaring war.

Astrology's popularity began to diminish around the 1700s. This was during the Enlightenment. Numerous publications were published that challenged the validity of the practice. Astrologers lost their place in the courts as well as in the homes of the average citizen.

Fast forward to the present day, and astrology has been revitalized. Along with New Age movements as well as the emergence of new philosophies or bodies of thought, astrology has seen a resurgence in popular culture.

When you combine the popularity and technology of astrology, the reach of astrology is greater than ever. Its practitioners have seen a revival in popularity.

Western traditions are now the most popular method of astrology. Most astrological interpretations and studies today are based upon Zodiac signs.

The Birth Chart

For the complete study of the stars, planets, and their signs and symbols, one piece is required. The most important clue in the mystery and art of astrology is the exact date and time of the individual's birth. All analysis is possible from this piece of data.

A birth chart is a record of a person's birthday and how it connects to the celestial entities. In simple terms, from the moment that you are born, all of your energy interacts, flows, and mixes with the celestial energies. This is what makes you unique and different. Each body in the cosmos has their unique and particular locations at the time of your birth.

The birth chart is also known as a "natal" or astrological chart. It shows the person as the center of attention in a vast network that represents the celestial objects. This chart freezes the motion of time, both on Earth or in outer space.

It trace the tracks and then immobilizes planets or stars on the specific place at which they were born. Astrologers need to know not only your date (complete with year, month, day), but also the exact location and time at which you were born to complete their chart.

The birth chart is populated with the exact locations of all the objects in space, including the sun, moon and planets. Astrologers will then draw longitudes and latitudes lines, position important celestial body, and do other calculations. The birth chart has been completed and is ready for interpretation. The chart's distribution and locations often provide the basis for an analysis. Astrologers might also look for patterns or unusual places that provide information on the person.

This was the case in the pre-modern era. The only people who had access to birth charts was the elite and royalty. During these times, the average person won't be able pay enough to have his own birth chart created. But today, birth charts have become more accessible thanks to modern technology.

Before you start reading this guide, make sure you have created your birth chart.

Astrology, Wicca religion

Wicca is a modern religion but has old roots. Gerald Gardner, an American anthropologist/archaeologist, introduced Wicca to the public in 1954.

He wrote many Wicca texts and traditions. He traveled extensively back when the UK was still an extensive British Empire. He lived in several colonies like Madeira, Sri Lanka, Malaysia. He also lived in Cyprus until his retirement.

During his homecoming he was introduced to a prechristian coven and was then initiated to it. This coven has survived to the present time.

He transformed the faith of his coven and added an holistic approach to it.

He also included the philosophies, practices, and scriptures he'd discovered through years of researching magical texts around the globe. This helped to create modern Wicca.

This is the accepted history Wicca. But, it is believed that Wicca is a manifestation of core beliefs which predate modern society. Its roots can be traced back from the Celtic clans and builders of Stonehenge in Britain.

Any practitioner who participated in the persecution of the Roman Catholic church through the Inquisition was exterminated.

This assumes that the patriarchal or masculine-dominated Christian faith was endangered by the matriarchal beliefs of Wiccans.

Wiccan circles have a lot of interest in astrology. However, the two primary celestial bodies that should be observed are the sun and the moon. This is a key factor in the changing seasons as these bodies have been scientifically proven to alter the seasons.

These celebrations can take place in many ways according to different traditions. Some traditions celebrate four major holidays, others six, and some Wiccan branches even have eight major festivals. These are known as sabbats. These sabbats take place according to the seasons, moon phases, seasonal changes and other changes.

There are many names for the Wiccan branches. Gardner used English names as the main celebrations. Some others used names from ancient Celtic traditions or common names that refers to the activities such as Harvest Festival.

Many Wiccans today prefer the Celtic names of these seasonal holidays. Minor holidays are celebrated around the equinoxes, solstices.

They are usually named using German names for pagan holidays. However, the names bear little to no resemblance the German practices.

Many influences influence these rituals and practices. Some even draw inspiration from holidays celebrated by the wider cultural community. These celebrations, which often involve the same festivities, are not repetitive or redundant. Instead they form as part the moment and follow a loose guide specific to the particular Sabbat.

Each celebration is associated with its respective associations. The result is a very complex system designed for maximum magic power.

The heavens have been leading humanity for as long time as we know, and astrological practices can tap into that magical power. It is thought that the planets each have their own impact on Earth.

Magical Victorian groups as well as older ones used the hermetic idiom, "as higher than so below", to their slogan. It is a good idea, naturally, to be familiar with these energies in order to better navigate the earth's life.

Astrology is complex but can be used religiously, or simply to keep track and maintain time and dates. Each planet has its unique attributions and governance of earthly events. This is how you can navigate magic on Earth.

You may want Venus to perform a love spell or Jupiter to aid you in your financial matters. Whatever your purpose, astrology has many benefits. You can use it to help you time your rituals properly and harness the energies of the heavens in order to make your life more enjoyable. Astrological timing, one of the most efficient and effective uses ofastrology, is one.

These techniques are used for planning and timing events that align with the positions of planets. This creates positive planetary energy which will increase the probability of an event's success. The celestial occurrences are already incorporated into time plans and other aspects, so it makes sense to use them for our benefit.

An app or an online resource can help you determine the positions and times of the planets. It depends on the event and the nature of it, you should ensure that the planet responsible for the event is in a favorable location to ensure the event's success. This practice can be aided by the following planetary attributions.

Candle magic may be connected to astrology or other elements, but can also be used alone. Candles with a particular colour can be linked to specific planets or element. You can also write prayers or sigils onto candles to perform magical operations. This kind of magic can be traced back as far as the Paleolithic era.

There are many variables involved in performing any type of magic. To practice candle magic, you will need a sacred space or a place that is unassisted.

A special place is needed to put the candles. Incense is used by many people in their candle magic.

You can use any kind of candle, provided it is clean before lighting. Avoid using novelty or chemical scented candles. Use a cleansing ritual to clean any candle. Use a fitting oil to dress the candle for the working. Simply use the following phrase to consecrate your candle.

This candle will be consecrated and cleaned by me in the name of the eternal goddess and the horned. This candle will only be used for good. So, may it so.

You can change this phrase to your taste. Use your imagination and make it unique. After consecration you can declare your purpose to the candle.

Inscribe onto the candle using your magic knife, sword, or sword. Inscribe from the top, middle, and bottom if you want to attract something. Inscribe from top to bottom if you want to repel an object or person.

One of the greatest benefits of astrology is its ability to plan and time events according to the positions of the planets. If you are planning ritual timing, it is important that you choose a favorable position for the planets so that your ritual can be performed in a timely manner. Venus must be in a favorable location if you wish to cast love spells.

Jupiter is your governor if you need financial help or want to succeed.

There are many ways you can calculate the timing of planets. An app or website is the best option.

Whatever your ritual may be, there are planets that can help you achieve the desired outcome.

You can also use the moon phases to help you time your rituals. This is particularly true when working with the goddess. However other rituals may also be timed using moon cycles. The full moon is often used to host large ceremonies and celebrations, particularly initiatory rituals. A new moon is used frequently to time fasting rituals and cleanses.

Properly timing your rituals will ensure there are no unexpected occurrences which could hinder your magical process. Our rituals can be synchronized to astrological events that will enhance our magic's power. This is how we ensure a successful practice.

Numerous plants and herbs can be associated with astrological signs. These plants are great to have if you want to gain favor with a particular planet. The appropriate herbs can be offered as offerings or burned as incense.

You can use these herbs in teas or smoking mixtures to help you align with similar astrological energies. Even a bath using these herbs can help you to be in tune with a certain planet.

Chapter 2: Planets (The importance planet sun, moon and all other planets).

The Sun

Your sun sign will be determined by the constellation where the sun was at that time. This sign represents the most fundamental aspects of your personality and is the one that people are most interested in. This includes your ego and inner self. All other planetary sign depend upon this sign. Astrologers liken your Horoscope to a painting. The sun sign, in this example, is the outline of the painting before the actual painting begins. It is important because it sets the foundation for how the painting will look. However, it is not complete.

The Moon

The Moon is the color palette. The Moon is just as important as your Sun in your birth chart. The moon sign shows how you feel emotions, and how you share them with others. The moon sign is a description of parts of you you don't realize are there. It also includes little habits you perform every day. The moon sign reveals your most basic needs of affection and how much you love the most. Because the Moon is associated with femininity, fertility, and love, it predicts a person's relationship with other women. This is not as romantic as Venus's relationship with Venus, but is more likely for interactions with mothers.

Mercury

Mercury controls our intelligent side. It predicts our rationality, or lack thereof. It influences our abilities in writing, speaking, and memory. Mercury can often have an impact on our ability to learn and how we take in information. Understanding a child's Mercury sign is very useful in understanding their school performance and how they can be helped.

Venus

Venus shows us how to love others and how to feel loved by them. Romantic relationships are often more challenging than those in normal relationships. The power we have to love and romance makes Venus a powerful planet. This planet not only affects your love life but also influences how you see beauty. Venus's sign is often responsible for your tastes in art and beauty. This planet is also famous for its love of pleasure. This planet can connect to what you love to do for fun. It predicts the ideal woman because of its feminine strength. This is typically the type of woman a woman wants to be.

Mars

Mars is the most in control over physical actions. Venus has an influence on the spirit of people, while Mars is more closely attached to the actions. Mars can predict your sex drive or preference for love, which is often predicted by Venus. Mars is the spark behind sex and the anger before a fight. It also represents the energy before a nation. Mars is the commitment before it happens. These are extreme examples but Mars is an extreme world. Mars could be the cause of any rash decision you have made that is not consistent with your normal processes.

Jupiter

Astrology views Jupiter as a sign of optimism and luck. Your life will determine how much luck you experience. As individuals, we experience luck in different areas of life. One who is gifted in wealth may not have the same ability to be beautiful or wealthy. Jupiter may represent luck, but it could also be lucky to you depending on your constellation. This planet also controls our philosophical views of the world and our feelings about deeper, more practical knowledge. This planet also predicts the areas where you may spend most of your life's time. This is how it identifies the things that are of greater importance to you than others.

Saturn

Not all planets promote positive qualities associated with their sign. Saturn was traditionally viewed as the "evil" planet. It is possible to see why this belief is held. Saturn is responsible for maintaining balance in the Zodiac. This can sometimes be translated to being "evil" since Saturn is often required to deny the excesses caused by other planets. People often interpret Saturn's denial as the destruction to dreams. This belief is only superficial. But if we dig deeper, it is possible to see that Saturn is actually the catalyst for human motivation. Saturn's ability to cause difficulties in a person's life can actually be motivational seeds that help them achieve their goals. Saturn's rule can be described better as "tough love" than "evil".

Transcendental Planets

Neptune (Uranus), Pluto and Neptune are collectively known as the "Transcendental Planets", since they aren't part of the original planets used in traditional Astrology. Traditional Astrology focuses on the planets visible to the naked eye. This doesn't mean these planets are insignificant. Because these planets are so far away from Earth, their impact on people is smaller. These planets often have higher levels of philosophical energy than the main ones. It is easier to see their effects on people if you look closely.

Uranus

Uranus promotes the uniqueness and energy of a person. It also encourages an affinity for quick ideas and creative solutions.

Neptune

Neptune powers our desire for escape. Neptune drives us to escape the everyday stresses by allowing us to read long books full of magic adventure and enjoy time alone.

Pluto

Pluto's slow orbit means that many generations share the star sign of this planet. This planet is frequently associated with the similarities of generations.

These are just some of the basic information about the impact of these worlds. However, there are many moving parts to a person's chart.

Example of a Birth Diagram

Name: Joe

Oct. 8, 1962, date of birth

Time: 4:00 AM ET

San Jose (California)

1) In order to start your birth charts, you must know your exact time and place of birth. If you don't know the exact time and date of your birth, it will be difficult for you to identify the ascendant in your sign.

2) Knowing where the constellations and planets at specific times and dates is essential in order to begin calculating your Birth Chart. This part is not easy for someone with a basic knowledge of Astronomy. A professional astrologer, or a website, may be able to help you find your signs for the birth chart.

3) Most birth charts have a table that lists the exact positions of each planet in each sign. From left toright you will see the coordinates, sign, and planet. The constellation the planet is in is shown by the sign to the right. This is where you will find the traits of your personality. These coordinates show the exact location of the planet in astronomy.

Sun in Libra

The sun is the essence of your personality, how you manage your day-to-day life and most basic expressions of your personality.

Aquarius Moon

Moon sign is indicative of unconscious emotionalism or moods.

Aquarius, as a sign of the moon, leads to extraordinary abilities in observation. Although they may not always express their interest, these people are extremely interested in the reasons for human actions. These people can be perceived as shy or detached, particularly during childhood. They enjoy being around people but often feel different from those around them. In their youth, these people rebel against their parents and become very proud of their children. Lunar Aquarius' become more mature and see unpractical and messy emotions as incongruous. They can take on almost any belief or opinion of their loved ones. These people are skilled at putting aside differences in order to benefit their family no matter what their ideals may be. These people can be stubborn about certain aspects of their behavior and character. These are people who won't listen to anyone and will do whatever it takes to get the job done.

Mercury in Libra

Mercury influences how we communicate.

Mercury in Libra has brilliant judgement because they take into consideration all options before making decisions. This individual may feel more confident when making decisions. They are able to communicate their views clearly and concisely. This person listens carefully to all arguments and points out potential problems before taking a decision. Even after making a decision, they may sometimes prefer to say, "Well, I'm kind of in between both ideas," or something similar.

Venus in Scorpio

Venus rules how we deal with romance and how much we value beauty.

Scorpions with Venus are more open to commitment and can attract strong partners. The attraction of this sign lies in their intense loyalty and dedication. This person is not looking for fast, fun, and easy relationships.

Mars in Cancer

Mars is responsible to the engagement in action and energy.

The combination of this sign with this planet leads to passive-aggressive tendencies. Although these individuals are known for their calm approach, they may be more inclined to display explosive emotions if they feel threatened. These individuals are strong because they have patience and prefer to wait until the right time to attack.

Jupiter in Pisces

Jupiter is responsible for our happiness and success throughout our lives.

The best fortune is for someone who gives back to the community. Good luck is possible for this person if they are charitable, generous, and compassionate.

Saturn in Aquarius

Saturn is the source of inspiration and how it's used.

Unless their family can't support it, they will be fully committed to their studies. In such a situation, the individual will do all the work and learn in a real-world setting. This person is focused on the work. They may find it enjoyable to spend time with people with more life experience and learn about the rest of the world.

Uranus is in Virgo

Looking for unusual solutions to problems?

Scorpion Neptune

It is not important to focus on the mundane. Prefers to be surrounded in practicality.

Pluto in Virgo

Individuals are able to easily collect information.

Ascendant at Virgo

The Ascendant is a sign of how someone will behave in his or her life. It also represents how others will perceive you and your attitude towards it.

Individuals who are Virgo Rising tend to not care much about their appearance. This person may seem shy or reserved depending on who they are around. These people also have a keen awareness of their bodies. They excel in many sports that require body awareness, like dance, martial art, or gymnastics. These signs pay attention to details and may notice things in situations others would miss.

Chapter 3: The elements: Fire, Earth, Air, Water

These four elements form the zodiac. The elements also work in harmony within us as do the luminaries and planets as well. You can also find all the elements within yourself.

Each element has three signs that are connected to it. The dominant element in a horoscope is a direct indicator of how a person behaves, reacts and responds. A chart that only analyzes the elemental balance can reveal much about a person's primary traits.

The elements are further divided into three modalities, as follows:

Cardinal Fire is Aries

Taurus: Fixed Earth

Gemini: Mutable Air

Cardinal Water is Cancer

Leo is fixed fire

Virgo stands for Mutable Earth

Libra is Cardinal Air

Scorpio is fixed water

Sagittarius can be described as a Mutable Fire

Capricorn is Cardinal Earth

Aquarius is Fixed air

Pisces can be a Water Mutable Sign

Mixing the elements with the modes gives us more insight into the primary traits of a person. Gemini, for example is mutable, and thus more likely to be very adaptable. Libra, however, is cardinal, and more likely than Libra to invent new ideas.

CARDINAL MODALITY

The cardinal modality (the first of three modalities) is the most important. It's associated with the four signs that start each quadrant, Aries through Cancer, Libra through Capricorn. Libra and Aries are day (or inhale), while Cancer and Capricorn signify the night (or exhale).

Since modalities refer to the basic mode in which a sign operates, all four cardinals signs initiate energies that open up a new season or stage in one's life. Cardinal signs enjoy starting new projects. They are the pioneers in the zodiac, but they can lack the persistence to bring their ideas and projects to fruition.

Pisces. Gemini and Sagittarius represent the day (or inhale), signs, while Virgo (or exhale), signs are Pisces and Virgo.

Mutable signs are, as the name suggests, flexible, adaptable, versatile and changeable. They can often see all sides and adapt well to change. However, they may lose focus or feel disoriented and can suffer from "shiny objects syndrome" and other distractions.

The Medicine Wheel is the Horoscope

The cardinal signs and elements have been used for millennia in shamanic cultures as the medicine wheels, which represent the four cardinal directions. Cardinal Aries (fire), cardinal Cancer, water, and cardinal Libra (air), are the first signs of spring in the northern part of the hemisphere. Cardinal Capricorn (earth), starts winter. These roles are reversed in southern hemisphere.

The four directions signify stages in life, including birth (east, fire and new beginnings), youth and adulthood (south, waters, emotional innocence, trust), old age (west) and older (north, sky, wisdom). The entire horoscope could be viewed as a medicine wheel and sacred hoop of the life that one can align with. You should note that this is just one way to view it. Different shamanic traditions have a different perspective.

The seasons of the calendar align with the

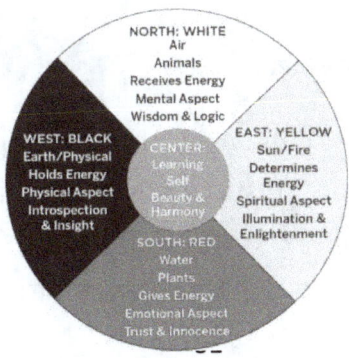

seasons that correspond to life's stages: birth (Spring), youth and adulthood (Fall), as well as elderhood (Winter). Everything is interconnected in the great mandala that is creation.

FIRE

Fire is the energy for transformation and action. To draw life's energy, we must inhale it. Also, our lungs expand upon inhalation. Fire signs and planets signify that our lungs are expanding. Fire is heat and movement. The energy of flames is what gives fire its name. Watch them dance and flicker, and you'll feel it. The Sun provides the Earth with the heat, light and energy that we need to live.

Fire is fast-moving.

The three fire signs, Aries, Leo, or Sagittarius, are positive, optimistic, enthusiastic, and self-confident. They are more closely associated with day energie, which is more directed and focused outwards, but all signs contain some fire power within, as all elements come in different amounts.

Aries is ruled by Mars, the warrior god of war, and is the first sign of the fire signs. Leo is ruled the Sun. He is assertive and loves attention. Jupiter rules Sagittarius. It is expansive and ingenious.

These traits can be attained by placements, luminaries as well as planets, asteroids and angles in fire sign signs. Aries has Venus (values/love) and is therefore more direct and warier-like. Mercury (the mind and communication), Leo people have a style of communication that conveys authority.

WATER

Water is the energy of emotion and receptivity. Water, just as emotions, can be fluid and shifty. Water constitutes a large percentage of our bodies and is considered to be the most vital element. Pisces is the water sign. Scorpio, Cancer, and Pisces all possess creative and intuitive energies.

Moon rules Cancer. This sign is associated with nurturing and mothering. Pluto rules Scorpio. This sign reflects the depth of Pluto and is associated to obsession and psychological depths. Neptune rules Pisces. He is associated both with all altered or meditative states and the connection to the collective unconscious.

Water signs give off a more fluid energy. Mercury (the mind & communication) in Cancer can, for example. They receive information instinctively, and they retain it at a deeply level. Cancer has a high receptive energy at night.

AIR

Air is the energy in your mind, or thoughts. It can also be called day (inhale), energy. This is both the breath or the wind. We cannot hold onto breath. It flows in & out. Wind is needed for the movement of air around us to prevent it from becoming stagnant. Gemini and Aquarius are the sign of the air. They represent thought, ideas, sociability and analytical. Air signs can be associated with logic and the right-brain.

Mercury-ruled Gemini is associated learning and duality. Libra, ruled Venus, is associated diplomatic work, mediation, and the maintenance of relationships. Aquarius is ruled and associated with Uranus. This is because it is connected to thoughts, ideas, people, higher intellect, inventiveness, and innovation.

Air signs are known for their airier flavour. Gemini has Mars (drive & will) and is known for being a fast learner. This person is also likely to communicate very clearly and quickly.

EARTH

Earth is energy, the energy of the physical world. Energy that you can feel and touch. Earth is stable and practical. It also has a lot of patience. Capricorn, Virgo and Taurus are the earth signs. These are the signs that signify hard work and the ability to create and connect with the physical world.

Earth signs can be sensual, have creative properties, and are linked to the natural cycles, as well the human cycle, of birth, life and death.

Taurus, ruled Venus by, is most connected to both the physical world and the Earth. Mercury-ruled Virgo has a stronger connection to the technical world. Capricorn is ruled over by Saturn. This sign is the pioneer of the earth signs.

Any placements made in earth signs will have the same flavor as the sign. A Taurus with Mars (drive & will) will be slower than someone who is in Aries with Mars (rule and rulership), which is quick-moving and direct.

Chapter 4: The houses (how calculate ascendant, 12 houses)

Concept of Houses

The House in astrology is usually similar to the time. Zodiac Wheel comprises twelve houses that are equally divided, and each house is ruled under a particular sign and planet. It runs counterclockwise. It is commonly called bhavas (in Indian astrology). The first house rises at 90° from the nine o'clock point, which is known as the eastern sky and is referred to the ascendant. The seventh house, located in the three o clock position which forms the western-horizon, is situated opposite. It works on the principle of Sun rising in east and setting in west. Each house occupies the 30-degree position in the zodiac wheel. This is illustrated in the following diagram:

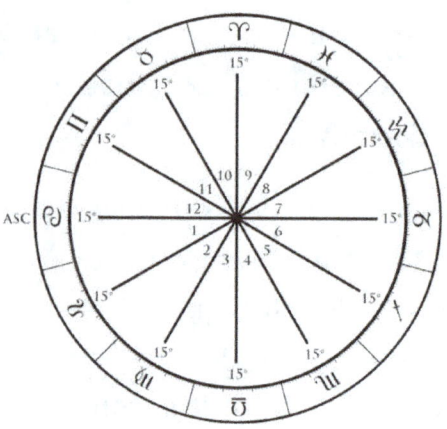

Illustrating houses and divisions

The middle-noon position in the Zodiac Wheel represents the beginning and end of the tenth houses. This is known as mid-Coeli. This 6 o'clock position is imum Coeli. The formations of the eastern, western, northern and southern horizons are also predicted by a zodiac wheel. Astrologers can predict the house by knowing the time and date of one's birth. Each house represents an individual's character and relationship to the Planet.

The Twelve Houses

What are ascendants?

The ascendants can be described as the zodiacal sign which rises from the eastern edge of the zodiacal circle. Based on the time and place of birth, ascendants are predicted. It was believed that an ascendant would reflect a person's physical appearance. The ascendants choose the zodiacal sign as well as the ruling Planet. This also influences the personality of an individual. Astrologers generally believe that the rising horizon or ascendants is as powerful as the Sun.

Calculating Ascendants

It is possible to calculate the astrological ascendants by using these formulae

$l = \arctan(x/y) = (-\cos thL/\sin thL + \tan th \sin e)$

The thL refers to the local time at degree and e to the Earth's inclination.

Take the value e 23.4492911o

If the ascendant's value is 180o

This will make it equal to ascendant +180o

And if you have xth

Then ascendant equals ascendants + 360o

A software program can also be used to calculate ascendant value. The following diagram will make this clearer.

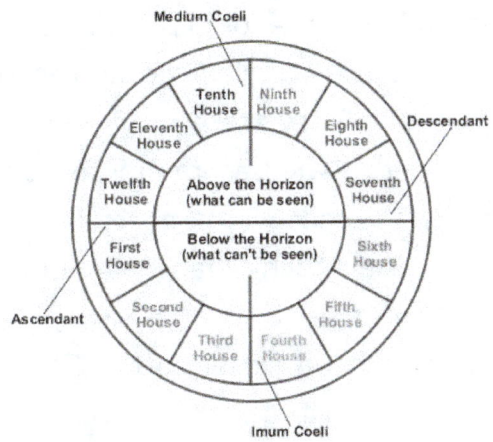

The location of ascendants, medium Coeli.

Effects on Ascendants

A variety of factors can have an impact on the ascendants. As the Sun rises eastward, it is believed that an individual who lies on the eastern horizon is more powerful than one who lies on the west. This will show the individual's personality. The influence of ascendant is thought to affect the first house. The strength of the opposite sign is automatically affected if the ascendant falls later in any sign.

Ascendant & Planet Relations

The ascendants are directly linked to the planets. The Planet rules the Zodiac sign of the ascendant. They are equal in importance to the Planet. It will become more obvious if you look at the following aspects. If Leo is the ascendant, their ruling Planet would be Sun. The chart ruler will be Sun. A rising Planet is one that is located closer to the first house. The ascendant will also have significance if the Planet is in close conjugation with it. The ascendance is in direct relationship with the Planet.

The Aspects

Aspects are the angular relationship of Planets. They are useful in explaining the path of energy. Astrologers interpret a person's birth chart by predicting where a Planet will be in relation to a sign or house. Astrologers also assist in the prediction of the relationship between Planets. The factors can be described as follows:

Conjunction, which stands for 0 degrees, is what determines the powerful combination two Planetary energys. It occurs when Planets are closer to one another. They even share the exact same degree as their sign. The conjunction can be considered the first house aspects because the Planet will be in the exact same house. Their energies merge, which can result in mutual benefit to the individual.

Sextile- Refers to the 60 degrees angle. This is related to opportunity and experience. It points to the formation of new relationships. It is formed at 60 degrees from the Planet. The sextile follows a relationship of three by eleven type. To give an example, if Planet Mercury (at 15 degrees Taurus) is located in the chart and Planet Mars (at 15 degrees Cancer) is located, then they can be considered in sextile attributes. Planet Mars is located in the third place from Planet Mercury (at the 11th). In this case, it would be expected that they will manifest one another and be involved with group activities, communication, etc.

Square - 90 degrees is the equivalent of 90 degrees. This signifies potential, challenge or constructive period and focus. It is created by the Planet at 90°. Any sign that falls within the same cross is considered to be square. It is also called the "four by 10" type of relation in that the Planet is either located in the 4th or the 10th house.

Trine, which is approximately 120 degrees, represents creativity, vision, ease of inflow, cooperation and experiences. The sign of this aspect belongs the same Elements. The 9th and 5th house types of relationships in the trine share many of the same qualities.

Quincunx: This expectation is 150 degrees in angle. It assimilates contradictions and can transform potential power into adjustment in real and imagined life. This relationship includes a sixth and eight houses. The services, matters of health, obligations and debts, among others. This is a problem that sometimes manifests itself.

Opposition - Refers to 180 degrees. This created conflict in two opposite energies. It creates balance in integration, objective thoughts.

The Twelve Houses

The First House

The Planet Mars is the ruler of the first house. This house is self-oriented. It is also known to be the home of ascendants. Ascendants are those who rise from the east at the moment they are born and show an exceptional personality. This house is directly connected to the physical appearance of a human body. The Planet is the planet in the first house. It gives strength and importance. It is also known by the name "The ruler of childhood". The first house recognizes an individual's potential and contributes to his or her development as a person. Strong houses are a strength for the whole chart, and they also improve the quality of the overall quality. Without a doubt, the weakest house can reverse this idea.

The Second House

The rulers in the second house are Planet Venus (Taurus sign) and Planet Venus (Planet Venus). This house is sometimes called the possessions House. The second house owns all of the emotions, needs, self-capability and desires. Their second house can enhance their lives. Any amount we make, whether that's through investments, buying cars or clothes, is worth something. The second house owns all these things. The second house can address the individual's financial ability. The planet associated to this house controls knowledge and speech. The second house can also address financial reversal. This house is also associated to physical wealth.

The Third House

Gemini is associated to the third house. It is also known as "the communication house". Our daily activities. The third house is responsible for our daily activities, including routine, travel to places and communication with family members. They possess intelligence and an analytical outlook. Mercury is the planet's ruler. Its retrograde can keep you still at times. The third house rules our communication, education, and skills. The third house addresses our spiritual and psychological connection. The third-house has an exceptional listening ability.

The Fourth House

The fourth house focuses on the sign Cancer and is controlled by the Planet Moon. It is the home. The fourth house can be associated with a home association, where we can set our roots down to the earth. This house is about inner peace and self-centeredness. The fourth house is responsible for our physical and physiological activities. The fourth house is thought to contribute to analytical approaches and self-individuality. This house is associated also with the physical structure, real estate work. It acts as a bridge between individual and home life.

The Fifth House

Leo sign and controlled by the Sun, the fifth house is associated with Leo sign. The fifth house addresses creativity and inner confidence. It also controls leadership and self-realization. This house is associated for pleasure in an individual's life. The third house is associated also with children as a source of pleasure. The fifth house is focused on emotional enrichment and pleasure. This house is rich in financial pleasure. It also appears to be the controller for the hobbies we have in life. Gambling, which can sometimes bring financial risk to a person's life, is also associated the fifth house. This house is also known as the human face, because it provides self-satisfaction.

The Sixth House

The sixth house, which is associated with the House of Health and Correspondence to the Virgo Sign and ruled over by the Planet Mercury, is the home of the sixth house. The sixth house helps to maintain a person's good health. The sixth house is responsible for financial loss, health issues, or fate reversal. The sixth and final house address our moral duties and prime responsibilities. The keys to the sixth home are quality of work and the provision of services. The sixth house teaches us valuable lessons about work and the benefits of services that are essential for our personal growth. The sixth house assists in maintaining one's strength throughout life. It helps us to appreciate work and the value of services. The sign and planet associated with the sixth House experience the struggles we face when we work. It can be helpful in maintaining physical fitness and a focus on work. Hygiene maintenance also comes under the responsibility of the sixth floor.

Prediction of house location.

The Seventh House

Libra is associated with the seventh House, which is ruled and governed by Venus. It is commonly known as the "house of partnership". This house is responsible for marriage matters and governs legal and business partnerships. The seventh house emphasizes cooperation and partnership. Venus, the goddess of the seventh house, represents the support of romantic relationships. The seventh-house is often responsible for the breakdown of relationships, such as divorce, violent partnerships, and even the death of a spouse. This house always felt the desire to improve the relationship. It also helped to improve the lifestyle. The householder Planet sign and the house sign indicate how experienced the couple is in a relationship and how they will approach the partner. Their darker side could make you enemies, or even create obstacles on your way to success. This also serves to teach us lessons at our best points, even when we are on our worst side.

The Eighth House

This house is associated both with the Scorpio sign and the Planet Mars, and Pluto. This house symbolizes the deep and dark sides of life like death and sex. The eighth house is sometimes a troublemaker for the Planet of the Eighth. This house is often linked to an individual's income and wealth. This house is also known as the house of sex. It can also bring on phobias and other negative effects. The eighth house speaks out about the importance sex and death. This is something that we all experience in our lives. The eighth house is also able to support career shifts and new relationships. The eighth house covers financial support, physical and spiritual connection. How will we manage our relationship? How we interact in relationships with others, and what type of qualities we have. Which personality traits have we brought into our lives? Are all concerned about the eighth.

The Ninth House

This house has been called the house where the philosopher lives. The ninth house is associated the the sign Sagittarius. It is ruled and governed by Jupiter. The ninth house handles the import and export of services goods. The character of the ninth house is similar to that of Planet. It is both a philosopher, and aspires to be one. The house shows a keen interest and passion for religion. This house is committed to moral, ethical, and social standards. This house can also be used to support long trips or travel to foreign countries. It is called the house for in-laws. It gives you the ability to grasp the theories. This will help you build a wonderful world. It can also be quite cruel at times. It encourages greed and has unneeded ambitions. It can also be fair and supports the growth of individuals. Understanding and accepting these things better is key to this house. It is most suited to philosophers.

The Tenth House

The tenth and final house is the one of social status. It is associated with Capricorn, ruled over by Saturn. It shows the individual's interactions with co-workers and the team. The tenth place is where you find your vocation. The tenth place is the home of our goals, our career aspirations, and many other aspects. This house also assesses the number of achievements we will make in life. Similar to the house first, this house also examines our achievements in life. The house it controls has a powerful social, financial, and financial position. This also relates to the type and profession that suits our house. It is also used to express self-identity, social status. This is where we address how to manage all the house's benefits.

The Eleventh House

Aquarius is associated with the eleventh House. This house is concerned with friendship and group activities. The rule of two Planets, Uranus und Saturn. This is the house of friends, which deals with our hopes & desires. This house is about wealth and represents the possibility of earning it. Social networking and organizational. It also speaks about destiny. The house also offers the gift of hardwork. It is our communication and effort that will bring us success. It helps us focus on the important things in our daily lives and makes it easier to do so. This house is known as a labor lover and is the strength for the eleventh. It is associated with the creativity of the mind. This Planet also has an association with adopted children. The house represents friendship and activities that will lead to success. This house might bring down their self-centeredness, sometimes to their worst.

The Twelfth Home

Pisces, the twelveth house, is closely related to this house. Pisces is both concerned with spirituality and sacrificial giving. This house is ruled planet Jupiter and Neptune. This house is known to bring positive change inside. It is sometimes called an unconscious house. This house creates hopelessness in you. This house also affects misfortunes such as withdrawal, loss, or enemies. This house deals with empathy as well as sensitivity. The key to this home is the spiritual connotation. Sometimes it causes confusion in the brain. With this house, you can find out the truth. It makes an effort to improve our lives.

This house, on one hand, deals with fate. It works on the principle Karma. This house is involved in charitable institutional work. It is connected to the learning from past and current, which helps us to move forward in life.

Chapter 5: Horoscopes: Transits and Horoscopes - Horoscopes 2020

Numerous people seek out astrologers to help them with their relationship issues, career changes, or opening new businesses.

People often make changes in order to improve their earning potential.

We will focus on income sources that are tied to other people's assets, such as bank loans or business partnerships, inheritance, gifted money, and other types of income.

We will look at the indicators within the natal chart. To demonstrate how Horoscopes can have a significant impact on your life, even financial, I will be using an illustration that I created. The natal configurations of the most sensitive to career and financial changes can be clearly seen by looking at one horoscope.

Let's take a look at indicators that indicate financial improvement in the Horoscope. We want to see transit activity from Jupiter, Uranus and Pluto in the eighth harmonic hard aspect. These include conjunction, semisquare (45 degrees), square (135 degrees), sesquiquadrate (135°) and opposition to the ruler of 2nd house (money and/or planets) located in the 2nd. Because the area of concern for other people's resource is the ruler and planets in the eighth house, we also want to be focused on them.

Jupiter is a good planet. It can enhance and expand whatever it touches. Uranus can bring new and exciting developments to the table, as well as sudden changes.

Pluto represents empowerment and transformation.

We are not interested to transit Neptune. If transiting Neptune happens to be in an aspect that is difficult for the planet ruling the 2nd House, it could indicate confusion, doubt, and insecurity.

Neptune in the hard aspect to Saturn ruling the 2nd, or 8th house is unlikely to be a positive influence. Saturn can be restrictive and controlling. We will therefore be focusing our attention on Jupiter and Uranus as well as Pluto.

We are interested in looking for solar transits from Jupiter, Uranus and Pluto in hard aspect with the angles of our horoscope. The Midheaven is an indicator of career changes, recognition and a change in status. Hard aspect to the planet located in the tenth house or ruling the 10th. As it is income-producing and a recognition from the profession, the 11th floor also has to be considered.

Pluto and Uranus are another important combination in solar-arc (SA) activity or transit activity.

Jupiter to Uranus or Uranus tying the knot with Jupiter suggest exciting opportunities, success and independence. It is optimism, which intensifies (Uranus), as well as the reward (Jupiter). Jupiter to Pluto or Pluto and Jupiter signify success, wealth, establishing opportunities, leadership, influence, and resourcefulness.

The reward cycle that transits Jupiter conjuncts Sun, is a twelve-year cycle. The reward cycle of transiting Jupiter conjunct the Sun is a twelve-year test that will reveal if there are any themes in someone's past.

It was, for example, that I had a business venture started every twelve years.

If Jupiter transiting conjunct Saturn does not bring you a reward, there are usually other factors that counter or negate Jupiter. This can include transiting Pluto to Saturn and transiting Neptune the Sun or angle in the horoscope.

Transiting Jupiter conjuncts Sun can be a sign that you are being promoted, rewarded, or recognized.

We also need to look for the transiting Uranus and Saturn, or solar arc. This calls for a wake up call. Imagine cheerleaders sitting on the sidelines watching a football match, jumping up and falling. It's now time to get things moving, to speed up the pace.

It can increase ambition and bring in exciting new developments. It could also be about making changes that give you more freedom or independence. Sometimes it's about freedom in relationships which leads to a breakup, but simultaneously, career advancements can happen. You can check your horoscope and find out what you saw when transiting Uranus (or solar arc) was in hard aspect to natal Saturn.

The solar arc measurement, which is transiting Saturn squared or conjunct the natal Moon, can also be used to track career progressions. This happens approximately every seven year by transit. This can be described as an advancement in one's career. This configuration is what Astrologer Noel Tyl calls "the architecture and advance".

This will enable you to identify which areas of life might be affected. It's a reliable indicator of career progress every seven year.

Similar is the Secondary Progressed Moon. This occurs about once every seven year. This is a great time to be ambitious in planning and strategizing. It is so strong, it kicks in usually six months before an aspect is exact, 6 months after exact – about one year worth of ambitious activity.

These four factors are critical for career advancement and promotion.

Let's look at a sample of your horoscope to get an idea of how it works. It will help you make better career decisions and improve your finances. It is amazing to see the solar arc develop and bring out the natal aspects. This is where the real progress occurs. I would like to show the sensitive areas of your horoscope.

The 10th house is first. The Sun conjunct the Midheaven was your birth sign. This means that whenever transit hits the MC, the natal Sun follows. They work together.

Transits will bring about changes in the profession or finances when Uranus and Mercury are struck off.

Venus squares the Moon at the 2nd House. The third natal aspect is Venus. Venus is the 11th house for career recognition. It rules both the Ascendant & 6th houses. It has significant significance when a planet rules a particular angle of the Horoscope.

Let's imagine that you were between 24- and 25 years old when you borrowed a loan to fund a business as computer consultants.

Jupiter ruler of Jupiter would be the associated bank loan. One of your parents was required to cosign the loan because you didn't have collateral.

When we look at the solar radiation first, we can see that SA Ascendant is conjunct with the Moon in 2nd house. In the second house, SA Jupiter was sesquiquadrate Mars. SA Venus was the ruler of the 8th and 9th houses, and SA Uranus had a hard aspect with the Midheaven.

Transiting Pluto was placed square the Midheaven indicating something large was at work. It's a volcano bubbling with hot lava that is about to explode. These are the events that are happening through this transit.

Transiting Saturn was opposed to the Ascendant. Transiting Saturn above the horizon through houses 7 through 12 signifies an increase in responsibilities to the outer world. You feel a release from the 14 years past when Saturn was below your horizon. The person is now clearly visible.

Transiting Jupiter was placed in conjunction with your Midheaven, Sun. Transiting Jupiter's relative speed would make it conjunct Mercury and oppose Uranus because they move very quickly.

Then it would oppose Pluto.

You can see the houses associated with this activity in right column: the 2nd house; the

3rd house (the Moon governs the 3rd), the 7th house; the 8th house; and the 10th house.

In continuation with our example: Around one year after you became self-employed, financial tension was growing. It was clear that your loan repayments would only be for a limited time and you were trying to expand your business by acquiring new clients. Let's assume that now, you are forced to work for another sales company while you build your own business.

We see SA Venus squaring Jupiter, and then the following year, SA Moon versus Jupiter. Venus square Moon now represents the natal configuration. This was the time that you began working for this company as a sales representative (Moon rules third), and your mother (Moon), assisted you in repaying the loan. This clearly illustrates the importance and power of mother (Venus square Moon), as well as 8th house resources (Jupiter). During that time, SA Uranus arced from the

MC to the Sun. The Sun rules over the 4th house.

You were working from your home office. Transiting Uranus was against the Moon, and square Venus. It was a time when the company needed to reprogramme itself. Transiting Saturn was in an aspect to the Moon of the 2nd place. Transiting Jupiter was square Saturn, square the MC and Sun, square Mercury, square Uranus. We see here that transiting Jupiter was sensitive to both career and finances.

If there is an opposition, conjunction, or square in the natal chart, such that Venus squares Venus, the Sun will aspect them both (at 23 Gemini and Venus) within one year. One degree equals one year of living in solar arc formation.

Same applies to the Midheaven's natal Sun. It can be seen in the aspect grid as two degrees apart, or two years apart for solar arc formation. Mercury and Uranus are about 2 1/2 years apart (32').

Let's not forget that you may have switched jobs in 1989 for more money in sales work, and your small business was still going strong. We see SA Uranus getting closer to the Moon. In 1990-1991 SA Uranus would face Venus.

It is an excellent combination, as seen in 1987-1988. 1989 was a successful year for SA Mercury as ruler of 2nd house. It was semi-square the Midheaven and transiting Jupiter was in 2nd house. All of these aspects are compatible with the essential natal configurations in your horoscope.

In 1990-1991 you made a complete change in all aspects of your life. Transiting Saturn was about to make a conjunction in the Midheaven. It had just completed conjunction with your Saturn Return in 1990, occurring in the 9th.

Around May 1990, you quit your job. You had decided to leave large corporations. You have decided to leave a country.

You worked in the areas of accounting, finance, administration. You were a SA Midheaven=Jupiter from 1990-1991 in your 9th place of internationalism.

SA Uranus was oppose Venus ruler of your ascendant. It's exciting to experience the exhilarating, thrilling change. Uranus rules the 10th house. It has 10th house concerns when it moves in solar arc development.

Saturn was opposed by The Secondary Progressed Moon. Transiting Saturn will be conjunct with the Sun's Midheaven. It's time for more responsibility and to reach the peak of one's career.

Transiting Jupiter was at the 4th-house cusp, where it was opposed by the MC or Sun. By solar arc or transit activity, a planet can bring a new feel to the IC (4th house cusp). This was a time of major changes in every aspect of your life. You were promoted quickly between April and Oct 1991.

1992: Transiting Jupiter was placed in conjunct Mercury. Uranus was the ruler of the 10th. The Jupiter-Uranus combination was successful. You were promoted to Europe and other parts the world. You were employed in two countries in 1992.

You were awarded the promotion that you had been striving for the past four year with SA Jupiter versus Uranus at the close of 1994. You were made financial controller. You had achieved your goal. Transiting Pluto, which was above the horizon, was opposed to the Ascendant. One can become more visible or empowered.

We also see transiting Uranus conjunct Saturn as well transiting Jupiter square Mercury, Uranus and Uranus. This time, everything sensitive to your natal chart is being activated.

The Ascendant was finally defeated in 1995. SA Mars opposed the MCC. In this year, you were promoted for work in a country considered a dream place. SA Mars ruling in the 12th place opened up the spiritual side to life.

You had personal experiences with the spirit world and otherworldly realms. We also see transiting Saturn squared by the Moon during this promotional. This was the last time it happened, in 1987-1988. It was when you first started selling. We also see transiting Jupiter opposed to the Moon.

You decided to leave the Club you had been working with to open your own business in May 1997. As it was when you first started your business as a computer specialist in 1985-1986, transiting Jupiter is again conjunct Midheaven & Sun.

Transiting Uranus means that it is close to a conjunction of the Midheaven/Sun. If transiting Uranus crosses the MC, it is possible to find self-employment opportunities or make professional changes that give you more independence. Transiting Jupiter will oppose Uranus by conjuncting Mercury. SA Mars would oppose Sun.

Initial plans were for you to start a small business with your father. But that didn't happen quickly.

There were disputes between us and SA Mars=Sun, our father, in the tenth house.

You moved (Mars) impulsively to another country (the Sun is the 4th), in the fall of 1997 to begin your business. 1998 was the year that Saturn squared the SP Moon. That was when you realized that the country was not right for you. You fled that country in the spring.

You were able to make a profit and sell the inventor you left with transiting Jupiter conjunct Venus. The intense drive to fulfill all your needs can be felt along with SA Mars= - Moon. Your finances are sensitive due to Venus' natal square and Moon's.

The 12th house was where Saturn has been transiting for 2 1/2 years. It felt uncertain about its future direction. It is time to get clearer about your career and personal goals once Saturn arrives at Ascendant.

The transiting Neptune conjunct with the MC signaled a change in profession into something spiritual, or alternative such astrology. SA Neptune was semi squared with the Midheaven, too.

You started the course in July 2002 with SA Neptune against the Moon, ruler the 3rd house. Transiting Saturn was placed in conjunct with the Moon, and transiting Jupiter was oppose to the MC und Sun.

You moved to a new place to conduct research on critical illnesses and spiritual heal. You also received financial support through your family which allowed you to devote time to research. SA Pluto was square Jupiter ruler for the 8th (other peoples' resources).

It was a time when new perspectives were important for the future. Transiting Jupiter, now conjunct Uranus within the 4th and opposing Mercury ruler in the 2nd houses, provided financial opportunities. 2005-2006 witnessed exciting developments. You launched your website.

We see the Accumulated Solar Arc Semisquare taking place in September 2005. Saturn was conjunct the SP Moon. Transiting Pluto was against the Moon, square Venus. Transiting Saturn was opposed to both the MCs and Sun. Transiting Jupiter was square Mercury or Uranus. Everything you had worked so hard for since Saturn in 2000 was conjunct Saturn's Ascendant, was now blossoming with possibilities.

In the second quarter of 2007, you began construction of a home with SA Midheaven=Sun. This is the ruler and fourth house. You created instructional videos and MP3 lectures in astrology around mid-2008. SA MC was squared the Moon, and conjunct Venus.

Transiting Uranus will conjunct Venus and square Moon in 2009.

Transiting Jupiter would join the Midheaven & Sun, then conjunct Mercury to oppose Uranus. This year will be a pivotal one for professional development, with SA Uranus=Ascendant & SA MC=Venus.

In 2009 you were granted permanent residency in a new country. The Midheaven represents our social status worldwide. We can see the same natal aspect configurations being hit on a consistent basis as growth occurs professionally and financially throughout your life.

Chapter 6: Numerology

Numerology is the belief of a divine, mystical relationship between numbers (and one or more life events) and numerology. Babylon and ancient Egypt are where the earliest records of numerology were found. There is evidence that the same form was also used thousands of year ago in Japan, China and Greece.

Life Path Number

Your Numerology readings will highlight your life path number as the most important. It will determine the course of your life. It should reflect who and what you are, as well as your personality traits. It also outlines the challenges or opportunities that you might face in your lifetime; it is also a representation of the lessons that may be learned in your life.

You calculate your life path number using your birth date. As an example, suppose your birth date was January 16, 1987. You can reduce this to a single number by adding all the numbers.

1+1+6+1+9+8+7=32

3+2=5

The life path number for you would be 5.

Life Path number 1

A life path number 1 indicates that you're dedicated and have creative ideas. Your natural tendencies are to reach the goals you have set. Your law of attraction gifts are about visualization and the creation dream boards. Your dream boards can be more powerful than verbal affirmations.

You may also find yourself on a constant quest to please others. This leads to you being unable or unwilling to prioritize the things you truly want in life.

Life Path Number 2

The life path number two is reserved only for those who are truly sincere and sensitive to emotions. These people try to be honest as a general rule, and they also avoid the temptation of ignoring their needs when making decisions.

These people feel like they're failing others, and that they're feeling defeated and helpless most of the time. It's possible to control this side by keeping a positive mind and not allowing it to manifest.

Life Path #3

Three means you are a social entrepreneur. Anything that involves people is easy. Number threes are great at romance and networking. You are optimistic for the future for the majority of your time.

There is also a flip side to this number. It is very difficult for a trio to focus on one thing and give their time and energy.

Life Path #4

Life path number fours have a practical personality and a strong Will. This life number believes in the law o' attraction and what people get from it. You like to plan before you actually do things.

On the other hand, they are more likiy to miss opportunities that arise spontaneously because of their structure. They are also less likely end up rich.

5. Life Path

People who were born with five lives are more likely be open-minded, flexible thinkers. They are more inclined to look beyond the box to solve problems. They are more in the present moment and less likely not to dwell on past events or worry about the future.

Five can also be self-indulgent. They will take pleasure in passing rather than invest in a long-term change. They are self-focused. They tend to channel their positivity onto others.

Life Path Number 6

This is the life path number six. It defines a true Samaritan. They are generous and compassionate, and can't help but spread goodwill wherever they go. They are kind and caring, and radiate love.

Sixes can also spend so much time giving that they find it difficult to take care of their own health. This leaves a six feeling that they are not capable of achieving the things they want in their lives.

Life Path 7

A seven-year-old life path is considered a reflective and peaceful person. They can enjoy connecting with others but they don't let that define them. Sevens already have the mindset to create a happy, balanced relationship.

Another side to seven is their difficulty in understanding the things they do have. They are less likely to believe in things they can't prove.

Life Path No. 8

A person with an eight-life path has a positive personality. They are determined and focused, but also have a good sense of what their surroundings are. They are organized and are confident.

The flip side of this number shows that they are too busy with practicality that they don't have time for dreaming. They often have trouble finding true and lasting love.

Life Path Number 9

People who have nine life paths generally get respect. This number indicates that a person is honorable and has a sense fairness. A nine is a number that has charismatic appeal. Other people are attracted to it. Nines have the ability to harness their magnetism and attract all that they desire.

The other nine side gets in the way quite often. They are very negative and obsessed about living the perfect life. They are often unable to achieve their goals because of these negative thoughts.

Expression Number

The expression number is also known to be your destiny number. It is used to determine your personal goals and abilities. It can also make you aware what traits you might be born with.

Your entire birth name is used in calculating your expression number. The Pythagorean numerology Chart is used to convert first, middle, or last names into numbers. This chart assigns an numerical single-digit value for each letter. Then, you add up the total and get one number. This is similar to the life path.

1

2

3

4

5

6

7

8

9

A

B

C

D

E

F

G

H

I

J

K

L

M

N

O

P

Q

R

S

T

U

V

W

X

Y

Z

Soul Urge Number

The number of your soul urge is also known by the number of your heart's desire. This number is derived only from your birthname and not the vowels. This number represents you as an inner person and can tell what motivates. This number is also capable to show you some of the reasons you make certain decisions.

It is important to be aware of when "y", which is a vowel, is derived from your name. If the vowel in your name starts with "y", it's considered to be a vowel. Your vowels are assigned a number. They are then added together to form an expression number.

A

E

I

O

U

Y

1

5

9

6

3

7

Personality Number

The personality number, in Numerology, is the number that explains your personality and the tendencies you send out into the Universe. This number will tell you what types of people are your favorite and why you are who you are.

It is very similar to the soul desire number, but using the consonants. Use the chart below to determine the numbers, then add them until they make a singledigit.

1

2

3

4

5

6

7

8

9

J

B

C

D

N

F

G

H

R

S

K

L

M

W

X

P

Q

T

V

Y

Z

Birth Date Number

Numerology simply refers to your birth date. The number of the months (1-31) in which you were conceived. Each number reveals a different trait which can help you gain insight into yourself.

1st

If you were born on a first month, you are a natural-born leader. You have a strong will and can easily gain the support of others. You are highly independent, preferring to work by yourself and not with others.

2nd

If you were born in the second month, you were blessed with a warm demeanor which is very useful for mediation. You are sensitive and yet have a diplomacy about dealing with those around.

3rd

If you were born in the third month of the year, you will be a natural-born musician and possess a high level of natural talent. Because of your loveable wittiness and demeanor, you are a social celebrity.

4th

If you were born on or after the fourth of each month, you are the perfect candidate for any employer. You are organized and meticulous with a good sense of empathy for family members.

5th

If you were born on a fifth month, you have a lot of wanderlust. You enjoy traveling and are driven to make your own decisions. You can adapt to almost any situation.

6th

If you were born on a sixth day of the lunar month, you are generous and family-oriented. You are kind and compassionate, and you can be a great peacekeeper. You are the person to call when you need to find the middle ground between a family feud.

7th

If you were born on or after the seventh of the month you will be very mind-oriented. You have great focus and intuition. You don't accept everything as true and you prefer to explore and contemplate all topics. You will often be able find the truth, even when others are not.

8th

If you were born in the eighth month of the year, you are a dreamer. Because you can dream up new ventures, you have the ability of taking a creative approach to your money. You are a problem-solver, a leader, and a good entrepreneur.

9th

You're a true humanitarian if your ninth birthday falls on a month. You bring with you an open heart and compassion for others. You are a charmer and have a natural ability to connect with people, regardless of differences.

10th

If you were born after the tenth month, you are extremely ambitious and seek independence. You have the desire to achieve your goals in every way possible. You are motivated by a strong sense success. This allows for you to rely heavily on your strong analytical mind, and strong managerial skills.

11th

If you were born in the eleventh month, you will have the ability to think positively but also realize that you aren't naive. Your dreamy mind can be matched by your ability and determination to be confident. Your intuitive nature helps you reach understandings for others.

12th

If you were born in the twelfth month, you are naturally artistic. You are creative in all aspects of your life, from your home to daily living. You enjoy expressing yourself. You are most likely the brightest person in your circle.

13th

If you were born in the thirteenth month, you will be the most reliable person in your community and family. You are meticulous and organized, and use these skills from work to your artistic endeavors.

14th

If you were born in the fourteenth month, you will be a person with a curious nature. Your nature is unpredictable and you will gravitate towards the unexpected. However, you possess an analytical mind and are able to communicate and interact with people.

15th

If you were born in the fifteenth month, it is likely that you have artistic talent. Strong instincts can be found in business and finance, but you also have the ability to communicate with others.

16th

You don't feel at home in real life if you were born on 16th of the months. You love to think big. You have great intuition, which is why you seem to be interested in the spiritual or philosophical realms.

17th

If you were born in the seventeenth month, you will be balanced by your ambitions as well as your financial and business skills. You have a practical sense of judgment that is inspiring to others.

18th

If you were born in the eighteenth month, you are a natural-born leader. But your talents also inspire those around you. You are a brilliant manager and politician because of your ability to get along with people. You have a wide mind and can communicate your feelings well.

19th

If you were born on or before the nineteenth of the month, your ambition is balanced by your independence. Your creativity and risk-taking nature are balanced by your creativity. Combining your creativity with your sensitivity will allow you to conquer any obstacle you face.

20th

If you were born in the twentieth month, you're a walking mood-ring. Everybody knows what you feel and how you feel. Although you are sensitive and strong, you must maintain a healthy distance with those around.

21st

If you were born in the twenty-first month, you have unique visions and creative thoughts that are fueled from your desire to succeed. You are passionate about what you do and how you treat others.

22nd

You were born on or around the twenty-second month. This indicates that you are driven and passionate about your profession. You are more creative in business ventures and less inclined to support the status quo. You are capable of seeing what you want and making that happen.

23rd

If you were born on or before the twenty-third day of the month you are flexible and easy going. You love change and take pleasure in taking on new challenges. While you have great skills in love and communication, your open mind is drawn to the possibility of something new.

24th

If you were born in the twenty-fourth month, you are highly family-oriented. You are a compassionate person who is willing and able to give of your time to others. This allows you to bring peace and balance to situations around you. Your strongest skills are in healing and meditation.

25th

If you were born on or before the twenty-fifth day of a month, you are blessed with a wide range of knowledge and understanding. You can make smart decisions. You are strong and balanced with intuition.

26th

You were born on 26th March. This means you have a bold mindset and a strong sense of finance and business. You can be confident and a capable leader if you don't lose sight the bigger picture.

27th

If you were born in the 27th month, your natural talent is to lead others by inspiring them. You have a great sense of organization. You have the ability to think creatively, which makes you a double threat. This makes you ideal for careers in art, politics and law.

28th

If you were born in the twenty-eighth month, you may be inclined to be a leader. But, only if there is good teamwork and cooperation. While you may seem rational and rational, your inner world is filled with idealistic and unconventional thoughts.

29th

If you were born on a twenty-ninth month, your imagination is heightened. Visualize your life. You prefer to use intuition to connect to a higher spiritual power.

30th

If you were born in the thirtieth month, then you are the true definition artist. You are charming and a social person. You are able to find harmony in all things you do. You must put in a lot of effort to find the right balance between your imaginations and your discipline every day.

31st

If you were born in the thirty-first month, you will honor tradition and your family. You want to build a solid foundation with those you love. Your natural talent to be drawn towards detail makes you a magnet for support and appreciation. You are always motivated to get the most from the opportunities presented to you.

Chapter 7: The Kundalini Rising

The Kundalini, also known by goddess power and serpent power, is believed to possess tremendous power. It is located at base of spine. The practice of awakening Kundalini is not only well-known in India but is also being used in other parts of the globe. The Kundalini, as it is called, looks like a coiled snake at the base the spine. Once awakened it can act as a gateway or key to great psychic abilities and even enlightenment.

Why is Kundalini so important to practice?

Kundalini awakening, which can bring you to a higher spiritual level, is an important skill to master. It is common for people to find themselves in a stagnant state in their spiritual journey. This is when there seems to be no development or progress. Awakening the Kundalini during this stage can often be one of your best decisions.

It doesn't matter if you are on a spiritual plateau in order to learn Kundalini meditation. It is possible to do this at any moment. This is the best way to get deeper into spirituality. If you're looking for a way to harness your psychic powers, this is the place. Kundalini awakening doesn't aim to gain psychic powers. Kundalini awakening doesn't require you to acquire such abilities.

Kundalini is good for your health

There have been many health benefits linked to Kundalini Rising. It promotes overall good health. It regulates and corrects blood sugar; it's an effective stress reliever; can fight or even cure diabetes and other illnesses; and has a host other benefits. It also provides relief for stomach and liver issues, as well as problems with gallstones or kidney stones. Even serious diseases such as cancer can be cured by awakening the Kundalini. When you feel the Kundalini power surge through you, you will realize that all things are possible. Clarity of thought is one of the many benefits of awakening the Kundalini.

These benefits can also be enjoyed without actually awakening your Kundalini. To reap these benefits, you will need to awaken your Kundalini.

Different Kundalini Meditations and Exercises

It is important to note that no one exercise or meditation technique can guarantee Kundalini awakening. For this to happen, it is necessary to practice spiritual growth and accumulate spiritual practices. It is important to apply that knowledge in daily practice.

Rising the Kundalini involves more mental effort and practice. Expect to meditate for long hours. But, you can also use physical exercises to help awaken the Kundalini. As such, any type of exercise can help to remove negative energies from the body. Your physical condition may dictate the type of activity you choose. Walking might be a good option. For those who are feeling strong and fit, you might consider running or going for a jog. It is important to exercise for your physical well-being. While some meditation techniques can directly engage and empower your Kundalini while others may only do so indirectly, It is worth noting, however, that all meditation techniques help to awaken the Kundalini. Therefore, you can rest assured your efforts will be worthwhile. Kundalini yoga can be considered one of the greatest yoga traditions. It targets and develops one's spiritual and emotional levels. It helps to raise consciousness, which can help one connect with a higher spirituality. It will help the mind and body become more physically, emotionally, spiritually and mentally strong.

It has been shown that when your kundalini energies are awakened (consciously or not), it rises from below your spine. This causes your brain to convert its power into vital hormones, and the 7 chakra centres undergo an amazing natural change. Potential psychic abilities may be possible that will allow you to increase your intelligence and predict your thoughts. Kundalini yoga offers six main benefits. These benefits include stability, strength, boldness. lightness. perception and isolation. It is your freedom to live a happy and strong life.

These are the benefits of kundalini yoga:

You get physical benefits.

Kundalini yoga can be a consistent practice that improves the nervous system. This will enable you to develop and create a buffer space in your mind that allows you to think clearly. Once you have achieved stress release, your pulse rate decreases, blood pressure drops, your muscle flexibility increases, your joints become more flexible, your digestive, endocrine or excretory functions improve, and your lung proficiency, cardiovascular efficiency, and lung proficiency increase.

You will also be able to strengthen your spine and make it flexible with the various kundalini movements. Many yogis, or observers, believe that age should not always be measured in terms of years. It should instead be measured in terms of flexibility and strength. Simply put, if 80 years of age and still tall, you probably look younger than any 60 year-old with a bent-back. Many kundalini activities focus on the spine. A lot of beginners are taught basic energy.

Kundalini yoga includes many breathing exercises. Deep breathing and Breath of Fire are the most commonly used. They help to increase and improve lung capacity. It is crucial to consider your lung capacity when you are feeling stressed, anxious, tired, excited, or angry. A low lung capacity will result in you gasping for air which will increase your stress levels and cause more damage to your lungs. Long, deep breathing is a key skill that will allow you to better manage your emotions and think rationally.

Kundalini yoga strengthens your core. Breathing exercises combined with leg lifts, stretch poses and other positions will strengthen your abdominal muscles as well as your navel center. This form of yoga tradition requires that you have a strong core. Apart from that, it's important to strengthen the chakra in your navel because it is associated wit persistence and willpower.

Psychological Benefits

Your awareness is the main goal of all types of yoga. In this form of yoga tradition, you are encouraged to elevate your awareness, which in turn improves your temperament, mood swings, overall well-being and self-acknowledgement. This will increase your self-awareness and decrease your tendency to become anxious, stressed out, or depressed. You will be able better manage your anger. Other than these benefits, your memory will be sharper, your concentration will improve, your learning skills will increase, and your social skills will be better.

Kundalini yoga has many meditation methods, but the one called "kirtan kriya" has shown significant improvements in memory. This has been recommended to Alzheimer's patients. It has been proven that it can effectively release stress from the body. Kundalini yoga's other important psychological benefit is its ability to provide peace of thought. While many people will focus on the physical and mental benefits of kundalini Yoga, the most important thing you need to be focusing on is your peace of Mind. Meditation is used in all types of yoga. One of the main purposes of meditation, whether it's for yogis or others, is to provide peace of thought. You will find your life becomes easier when you feel calm. If you can see the positive in situations and people, your life becomes easier.

Biochemical benefits.

Kundalini yoga has biochemical advantages. Kundalini yoga can help lower your cholesterol, sodium, glucose and triglyceride. It also reduces the number of white cells, which decreases hemoglobin, thyroidin, lymphocytes and serum protein.

When you practice kundalini, you should be focused on the benefits you get. This will keep you motivated and energized. But don't be so serious that you become anxious about practicing kundalini yoga. Take it all in, let go of all your worries, anxieties, and fears. Keep your attention on your breathing, your mantra and the sounds in your environment. You will find yourself happier, calmer. Your life will be easier, more productive. Your mind will be clearer. Positive people will gravitate to you if they see you as positive.

Kundalini activation's effects on the body, emotions, mind and spirit

It will improve your emotional state and make you feel more balanced. It will have positive effects on your emotional level even before you reach the stage where awakening occurs. You will feel less stressed.

Your mind will be more clear. You will be more able to analyze and think clearly. It will provide you with a level and depth of mental clarity you have never had before in your entire life. You will feel like you have complete peace of head when you experience this mental clarity.

How Kundalini feels

Your Kundalini may not be feeling as strong if it is still dormant. If your Kundalini is still dormant, you might not feel it at all. However, the more you work with it, the more you can feel it. A powerful surge of energy can be expected when your Kundalini awakening occurs.

This feeling is described as warm and warm. It is also a pleasant release. Some say it's even more pleasurable that having an orgasm. You could call it spiritual bliss.

How to get rid of the blocks that hinder Kundalini from rising naturally

Blockages can hinder the Kundalini rising and awakening. This can be prevented by making sure that the energy channels meridians are open to allow for free flow of energy.

What is the reason for these blockages, however? Blockages can occur for many reasons. Too much stress is one of the most common causes. Stress has become a very common condition in our modern world.

Unfortunately, this can make it difficult to have a healthy flow of energy. It is important to know how to manage stress effectively if you wish to activate your Kundalini. Although stress by itself is not harmful, it can be detrimental if you do not manage it correctly. There are many other things that can block the flow of energy. These include having negative experiences, emotional collapse, psychic attacks and others. When treating blockages it is important that you identify the primary cause. Common mistakes include not addressing the source of the blockage before treating it. It is important to address the root cause of a blockage, such as stress at work. The effect or result cannot be treated without looking at the source.

Clearing any blockages or healing needs should be done at two levels: the physical and the spiritual. Lifestyle changes may be required on the physical and spiritual levels.

How to awaken a dormant Kundalini

There are no specific rules or practices that guarantee Kundalini awakening. It all depends on your spiritual maturity, as well as your practices. There are two methods to awaken a dormant Kundalini. The first is by yourself. The second is with the aid of a spiritual mentor.

But if you wish to do it with the assistance of a spiritual teacher or guru, this will require complete devotion and submission. Some meditation practices may be required by your master. But, there are those who claim to be in a position to awaken Kundalini. It is hard to find a true master. Unfortunately, so many people claim they are masters but in reality are only full of hacks. The downside to this approach is the possibility that a master may be in a position to awaken your Kundalini. However, your soul may not have the capacity for it. This refers your spiritual maturity. You should do the Kundalini awakening work yourself. Although you may still need the assistance of a master spiritual guide, don't neglect your own spiritual development.

Chapter 8: Understanding Your Sign

Although you may be interested in your sign, it does not necessarily mean that you must study astrology extensively.

Aries

Aires can be represented by the ram. It represents male fertility, courage, aggression and strength. The horn of the ram is part the cornucopia. It is also known as the Horn of Plenty. This sign indicates an affinity for abundance.

Sun sign Aries people are natural athletes. They are energetic and direct. They are people who can see what they want and know how to achieve them. Moon can, however, play a crucial role in changing their behavior. Moon in Aries, for instance, is impatient. This means they are quick to react and don't have the patience to wait. This is why they are so proactive about solving their problems. They need to see results right away. These people are generally quick, competitive and direct.

Taurus

Taurus has always represented strength and power. Taureans have a reputation for being strong but also reliable and dependable. However, they can also be incredibly helpful because of their tendency to be outgoing. Taureans are naturally sensual, and take pleasure in comfort foods, blankets, and flowers. They love comfort and are open to material things. Because they are strong-willed, it is not wise to push them to do things they don't believe in. Once they are committed to doing something, they put in their best effort and time. This is why people who were born under this star love romance and love.

Gemini

Geminis are believed to be dual-natured because of the symbolism of twins. Geminis are often able to express their duality through interaction with other people. Geminis are adaptable and flexible, making them easy to deal with. Geminis who were born under this star have a tendency to be friendly, funny, and smart. Geminis can be more anxious under the lunar position and require more stimulation than most people. Sometimes they can become too bossy. Geminis enjoy being able to freely move and mix with people to find the answers they need.

Cancer

Because the crab is their symbol, those born under this star move in an indirect fashion. They aim to gain many advantages in their life. They are strong survivors. They are also extremely protective, particularly when it comes to sharing their inner selves with other people.

Cancers have a reputation for being moody. Cancerians are more inclined to be moody if the Moon is in Cancer. These people are often withdrawn, but they are also thoughtful. They can also be sensitive to love and give their loved ones a lot, such as comfort, security and care. Cancers can be very calm and quiet while they go about their daily business. They are gentle people who put their trust in their inner selves and make the best of it.

Leo

The Leo sign, which is also known as the Zodiac Sign, is symbolized by a powerful lion. This symbol represents power, leadership and courage. These people are characterized by a royal air. While they are considered to be dignified, Leo is also known for their conceit. Even though their exterior appearance is revealing of their conceit, Leo are driven by the affections surrounding them. Thus their plans often revolve around making people they care about happy.

Leo people love being the center and attention. Leos are always the center of attention. Their incessant desire to control things can be difficult to handle.

Virgo

People born in Virgo tend to be well-informed. The symbol of the Virgin is believed to symbolize purity of spirit and self-contained. Virgos can be reticent when confronted by something new. Virgos look for security and comfort in the simplest things. People with this sign are thought to be lazy and underachievers. The pleasure they get from the simple things keeps them from reaching for greater things in their lives. Virgo people can be a bit smug, even though this may be true.

Libra

The scale represents balance and is symbolic of those born under this sign. Librans have a great sense of sociability and are highly intellectual. Librans seek balance in their lives and have a tendency to be everything to everyone. They are also accused in their inability to be direct and take a strong stand on issues.

Librans strive for peace and harmony, so they are open to compromises and will let others win. Libra natives have the ability to balance their lives and are therefore very attractive.

Scorpio

Scorpions can be intense people. They are driven to succeed in whatever they set their minds to. They are motivated by power, so they have a lot more willpower. However, Scorpios are clever and very capable of navigating their environment. They don't grab things at the wrong time. Instead, they wait for the right chance. Scorpios are excellent at planning and scheming.

Sagittarius

Sagittarius are social and outgoing people. They enjoy freedom and dislike routine work. They can be dangerous because of their passion for friendship and blind faith in other people. Although they are optimistic, this can lead to them getting into trouble. Sagittarians under the fire sign are known for their quick tempers. However, they often forget where their anger came from.

Sagittarians require constant activity, and their outgoing personality makes it difficult to manage their time. They often forget appointments and find it difficult to finish tasks they don't love. This may seem like a problem, but they can be good teachers if they are good at storytelling.

Capricorn

People born under this sign are realistic and grounded. They also tend to be more determined about doing the right things. They have close relationships to Earth signs Taurus and Virgo. They want to be useful and productive in society. Capricorns value being productive and useful. They can experience turbulent emotions and are more likely to be skeptical with others.

Aquarius

Aquarius is the sun sign. Aquarius loves traditional ways of doing business. They are likely to hold strong opinions and have strong ideas. Aquarians are known for being standoffish, but this is a false impression. In reality, Aquarians are highly observant andtolerant in a wide sense. They are very intelligent and creative.

Pisces

Pisces encompasses all the experiences of all Zodiac signs. Because of this, Pisces is able to identify and communicate with people of all backgrounds. They are adaptable but also have broad minds. They also yearn for contentment. Piscesans often have a tendency to be dreamy because they desire contentment. They also glorify suffering.

Chapter 9: The History of Astrology

The stars have been guiding and guiding humans for thousands upon thousands of year. Stars were used long ago by travelers as a way to find their way, and ancient Egyptians relied upon the constellations and stars for weather predictions and forecasts. Survival basically meant that you had to adjust your daily routine based on the positions of stars and the times of year. Thus, it was possible to recognize the different cycles of nature, and adapt accordingly.

While this was practiced by many cultures, the Babylonians were first to make connections between pre-existing myths of the constellations and various philosophies. They also explained the twelve zodiac signs. Romans and Greeks adopted this system and incorporated it into the culture.

How Astrology evolved

The conquests of Alexander I the Great brought the Babylonian Astrological System to Greece. He traveled to Egypt, Asia Minor,

Greece and Asia Minor around 334BC. Along the way, he also shared his knowledge of other cultures including their cosmological beliefs.

These teachings were further developed by a Babylonian priest named Berossus, who traveled to the Greek island Kos in 280 BC. The priest taught his culture to the people.

The Greeks were open to the new knowledge. They combined Babylon's astrology systems with their own mathematics and philosophy.

These core techniques in astrology were first used in Rome and Greece. It was not long before leaders in Greece began to utilize astrology to their advantage. Roman emperors in particular used astrology to justify their authority.

The Tetrabiblos book, which contained the teachings, was created in AD 140. Claudius Polemy created it, which is the first book to cover these facets in astrology. Ptolemy wasn't just an author. He was also an astronomer, mathematician. These techniques form the basis of what is used in astrology today. However, astrology in the Western World was abandoned for 500 year after the fall of Rome's Empire in 476 C.E.

However, the Middle East was home to the Arabs who continued to learn, practice, as well as develop Greek astrology. This was possible because of the translation of Ptolemy's Book by the House of Wisdom at Baghdad. Astrology is preserved because of the Arabs. They also continue to develop it and see it as both an arts and science.

As it was integrated in various cultures, astrology flourished through the Middle Ages. Astronomers, doctors and mathematicians adopted it. These individuals worked together to advance the accuracy and detail in astrological charts. Numerous dominant figures like popes, monks or royal leaders began using astrology.

However, astrology's use declined once more between 1500s-1800s as religious entities became stronger. This was because groups such as the Catholic church sought to have more power over society and saw science, and skepticism, as a way for them to do so. Accordingly, they declared that astrology was not valid and sacrilege.

Fortunately, astrology gained a renewed interest during the 19th-century, as more people from Europe and England sought out to learn about mysticism. Carl Jung, a psychologist who was well-known for his integration of astrology into his patient evaluations, recognized the relationship between astrology (and people's) unique traits.

This reintroduction into astrology, which combines historical literature with contributions from different people, is for the most part what we use today. Thank goodness, we have more access to the teachings now than ever.

Astrology Basics

Astrology emerged centuries ago from the curiosity of our ancestors about the vastness, beauty, and power of the universe. They began to examine the movements of the moon, observe the sun's course, and to contemplate the infiniteness. Astrology and astronomy have been closely intertwined for centuries. They were both considered science. Astronomy concentrated on studying the sun, moon and stars. Astrology was more concerned with weather forecasts and natural events.

As astrologers grew more interested in studying the universe, they realized that the earth revolved about the sun through twelve cycles of the moon. They began to correlate the different patterns of stars in each cycle. This allowed them to identify specific climate changes that occurred.

The creation and use of the twelve months (with twelve zodiac signs), four elements, as well as associated personality traits, led to the creation the twelve months, twelve Zodiac signs, and four elements. This inspired the creation of the modern horoscope, much like the one that we use today.

The Four Elements

The four elements of fire, earth, air, and water were all considered to be the foundations of astrology in antiquity. These essential elements are still being used today. Astrology uses the element linked to a person's sign. It is representative for their primary traits and temperament. Each person requires each of the four elements to be present in their lives in order to experience happiness and optimal balance. Sometimes, in order to balance out the dominance of certain elements there is a tendency for people to gravitate towards those with them.

The element signs can be broken down into two categories: active or passive. Fire and Air are active signs that are self-expressive. Earth, Water and Earth are passive signs that are self-contained. This classification is crucial for compatibility. Fire and Fire complement one another. Fire is also compatible with Air and Fire.

However, Earth and Water elements thrive when combined in the same ways. This is because relationships sharing these dominating elements include deep understanding and nurturing each other.

Here are the characteristics for each element:

Fire

The Fire element symbolizes light and energy. Aries, Leo, Sagittarius, and Leo are all Zodiac Signs that fall under this Fire element. They are often described as being temperamental, self-sufficient, creative, spontaneous, and full of life. These people live by a strong ethical code and are known to inspire others. They tend to be very in tune with their gut instincts and are able to follow it without any hesitation. When they have strong beliefs, they are unstoppable.

Fire, like fire, can spark quickly and spread quickly. If it isn't contained, the passions that drive can quickly grow into anger. Earth and Air help to balance it. Water helps to reduce its intensity. Earth and Fire work well together. Fire may be leading the group, but Earth is most likely the one who formulated the plan.

Fire traits: Passionate, Enthusiastic, Positive, Inspirational, Spontaneous

Earth

The Earth element symbolises being grounded and responsible. People born under this element are Virgo, Taurus, Capricorn. These individuals are creative, hard-working, and seek stability. They aren't likely be involved in reckless acts or careless shenanigans, as actions are often well-planned and carefully analyzed.

They are able to create a safe space and provide assistance for those in need. However, they also enjoy the luxuries life offers, sometimes so much that it is considered superficial or materialistic. They are passionate about caring for others but they can be a bit numb to the feelings of others. Their strong will to achieve a certain outcome and their rejection of sudden change can cause them not to see how others are being affected.

Earth traits are: Responsible, Cautious and Sensible.

Air

The Air element stands for communication and charisma.

Like air, which is always moving regardless of whether we can see or feel it. People who are born under this element are constantly thinking and changing. These people are known for being quickwitted, and they are excellent problem solvers. Gemini, Aquarius (the Air sign), and Libra are some of the Air signs.

These individuals' personalities can be as diverse as the wind, and can range from outgoing to intelligent to scatterbrained to aloof. Air can lead to tensions in relationships. If someone doesn't agree, they won't join the crowd.

Air traits: Carefree, Charming, Independent, Inquisitive, Happy, Gullible

Water

Water is the base of emotions and understanding. Individuals who are born under the Scorpio, Cancer and Pisces zodiacs have a Water element. These individuals are often depicted as being sensitive and empathic and possess psychic tendencies. Due to their ability to analyze all aspects of a situation carefully, they are often seen as shy and distant. But once you have gained trust in someone with the Water element you will find one the most warm and kind people around.

These individuals may find it overwhelming to be able to hear what others feel, so they need to get some rest. If this tendency is not managed, it can lead to depression. Water element people can experience paranoia, overreacting to situations and hypersensitivity.

Water traits: Compassionate, Supportive, Sympathetic, Creative, Intuitive, Passionate

Astrological Signs Qualities

These elements are a key part of our personalities and inborn traits. However, the twelve zodiac sign can be separated into three types (or quadruplicities), that is, the Cardinal, Fixed and Mutable signs. Each grouping consists of four signs. They can be described as having dominant roles. Let's explore each quality.

The Cardinal Signs

Aries, Libra Libra, Capricorn and Cancer are the four Cardinal Signs of Astrology. They are known for their inborn ability to get things going. Coincidentally these four signs also correspond to the four seasons. Cancer is at the beginning, Aries at the end of spring and Cancer the beginning summer. Libra marks the beginning autumn. Capricorn marks the beginning of winter.

Aries' Fire sign is a laser-focused fire sign. It creates goals even when there are none. Aries excels at motivating others and creating momentum when they are in the leadership role.

Cancer's Water sign thrives off emotions. However this is not a sign to be weak. Cancer sign can inspire others and manipulate them to move towards the unknown by their strength.

Libra's Air Sign helps balance all the signs. They are open to new ideas and creativity, which will inspire, energize, motivate and excite.

Capricorn, an Earth sign, will inspire confidence and authority. Capricorn, a firm believer in the importance of getting the job done, has a knack for gathering the right people and is patient in reaching long-term goals.

Commonalities of Cardinal signs can be described to be instigators with the ability attract and inspire others to realize their goals. These individuals are extremely outgoing, have great leadership skills, and find great satisfaction in making things come to life. The Cardinal sign is a great way to ensure there is no time for boredom on your team, personally and professionally. These individuals are hardworking and enjoy inspiring others to make the world better.

The Fixed Signs

Fixed signs are Taurus and Scorpio as well as Aquarius and Leo. They are revered because they can turn an idea that comes from a Cardinal sign into a reality. People who fall into this quality category can be trusted, reliable, and are considered the doers. They constantly strive to improve their stability and progress, with strong steadyness.

Taurus, in the Fixed category, is the representative of Earth. Taurus must see tangible benefits in their progress. This could be in the form or money or possessions. Taurus will take care of their personal possessions, and also respect and protect yours. Taurus will never allow you to settle. He is determined to build and acquire items that last a lifetime.

Scorpio's Water sign is indicative of long-term success. This is achieved by gaining a deep understanding of others, and using that knowledge to inspire and motivate. Water is always flowing and changing, but it is essential for all life forms. It also relates to primal instincts and the unsolved mysteries and fantasies of imagination.

Aquarius is the element Air in the Fixed category. Despite not being associated with stability and being fixed by their easy-going ways they are extremely determined about maintaining their beliefs, building longlasting relationships, and maintaining a level of normalcy and protection.

Leo is the Fire sign. These bright and charismatic individuals love making people happy, using their creative and artistic skills, and displaying self-confidence. Leos have a tendency to not be afraid to convince friends, coworkers, and colleagues to believe and do the same things as them. They are also very determined and won't back down. Leo is a strong member of the Fixed type because of this firmness.

The Fixed signs will not quit. They won't give up even when something isn't working. They aren't known for being flexible and they can become frustrated or even petulant when they get overwhelmed. But their determination is what gets things done, even when others want to move on to the next thing. These people thrive on living in harmony with others and enjoy the feeling of accomplishment when they achieve a worthy goal. When you have a Fixed sign, you can be sure of dedication, patience, consistency and loyalty.

The Mutable Signs

Gemini and Sagittarius are the four zodiac sign that possess adaptable/mutable qualities. Virgo and Pisces are the others. These zodiacs signs can adapt to their environment and change their personalities as they please. They are often the bridge between people's ideas and their ideas. This is similar to the primary gear of an engine or conductor in an orchestra.

Mutable signs thrive upon change and are able to deal with stress, difficulties, and chaos with ease. Each mutable symbol has its own unique characteristics, just like every element or sign in the zodiac.

Gemini's Air sign, Gemini, is an observer of everything and everyone.

Sagittarius the Fire sign thrives from learning, experiencing new things whenever possible and searching for the truth and a deeper sense of everything.

The Earth sign Virgo helps others by healing and nurturing them, while also improving themselves.

The Water sign, Pisces, can also focus on others' emotions and adapt their responses accordingly.

Mutable signs are always looking ahead, preparing for the next change. A mutable will not allow you to forget anything by their intuitiveness. They will see subtleties in body language, patterns and body language. It doesn't matter whether you share specific details with them. Although they might appear innocent or foolish, they have many years of experience and can see through the complexities of your life.

They will always be there to help and are open to changing as needed. People who have mutable signs are usually very resourceful and they are loved by others. They often neglect their own needs in the effort to take care others. But, when they reach breaking point and give themselves time to recharge, they become as strong as ever. It can be very helpful to have someone who is flexible in your corner.

It is important to understand your element, quality, and the characteristics associated with it. The next chapter explains these characteristics.

Astrology has been used since ancient times by people from all walks. These components, along with the rhythms and cycles of nature, will allow you to get to know yourself better. This will enable you to be more successful in life's challenges. This will allow you to connect with others on an entirely different level and to reap the many rewards life has to offer.

Chapter 10: Astrology Sings

Each of twelve zodiac signs is representative of strengths and weaknesses, personality tendencies, attitudes, and other traits.

Below you will find the traits that correspond to each zodiac signs. You might discover commonalities about yourself.

Aries

(March 21 to April 19)

* Motto: "I Am"

* Symbol:

* Element: Fire

* Mars as the ruling planet

* Birthstone: Diamond

* Key Personality Traits

* Compatible Signs: Aries, Leo, Aquarius, Gemini, Sagittarius

* Recommended Professions

The Aries Personality

Aries-born people carry the zodiac symbol the Ram and are linked to the Fire element. Aries are recognized as the first zodiac signs. Aries individuals enjoy being first, and they are naturally born leaders. They are hardworking and competitive by nature. They are also self-disciplined and honest. Aries is an Aries sign. They are confident and kind-hearted.

Aries tends to be positive and optimistic. Aries have passion and drive, but that is only one aspect of their personality. Aries will get upset if they aren't happy. They will argue and show aggression which will quickly make an argument worse as their Fire sign ignites inside.

Aries is a friend, partner, and true friend. Aries are driven and energetic. They are creative and invulnerable, with a natural ability to think up new ideas.

* Strengths - Spontaneous Courageous Innovation, Courageous Courageous Self-Confident Leader

* Weaknesses

Notable Aries Celebrities Lady Gaga (Robert Downey Jr.), Reese Witherspoon and Pharrell Williams, Keira knightley, Zach Braff

Taurus

(April 20-20, May 20)

* Motto: "I Have"

* Symbol:

* Element: Earth

* Ruling Planet Venus

* Birthstone - Emerald

* Key Personality Traits

* Compatible Signs: Taurus, Virgo, Pisces, Cancer, Capricorn, Scorpio

* Recommended Professions : Entertainers. Chefs. Bankers. Interior Designers. Managers.

Taurus Personality

The Bull zodiac emblem represents Taurus and is representative of the Taurus zodiac signs. Taurus people have a charming personality and enjoy sharing their feelings and thoughts with others. Tauruses are calm, funloving and strong-willed. Taurus are not likely to get into conflict but they will resist being forced or rushed to make a decision when in unfamiliar territory. They are more likely to be slow and avoid making difficult decisions.

* Strengths

* Weaknesses

Notable Taurus Celebrities: Dwayne Johnson, Tina Fey, Al Pacino, Miranda Kerr, John Cena, Amber Heard

Gemini

(May 21 - June 20)

* Motto: "I Think"

* Symbol:

* Element: Air

* Mercury, the ruling planet

* The Pearl is the Birthstone

* Key Personality Traits

* Compatible Signs: Gemini, Sagittarius, Aquarius, Leo, Aries, Libra

* Recommended Professions : Computer Programmer, Advertiser, Auditor or Engineer

The Gemini Personality

The symbol of the Twins, which is the Zodiac symbol for Gemini, represents those born under this sign. They are charismatic, quickwitted and entertaining people. They enjoy intellectual conversation but don't discuss emotions.

Geminis are known as creative people who enjoy trying new things and being bored quickly. If they aren't challenged, their boredom can lead them to abandoning many projects. If they are bored with an activity or conversation, they will quickly quit and ask for help. If you are not interested in engaging in deep conversations with Geminis, don't bother to ask them. Geminis can sometimes be hard to live with and understand, but they are generally loyal and will take all necessary steps to restore stability. Geminis are often the glue holding a family together.

* Strengths: Communicative, Intelligent, Active, Informed

* Weaknesses: Illusive, Shrewd, Unpredictable, Trivial

Notable Gemini Celebrities: Angelina Jolie, John F. Kennedy, Marilyn Monroe, Johnny Depp, Naomi Campbell, Shia LaBeouf

Cancer

(June 21, - July 22,)

* Motto: "I Feel"

* Symbol:

* Element: Water

* Moon, the ruling planet

* Ruby is the birthstone

* Key personality traits: Romantic, supportive, vulnerable

* Compatible Signs: Cancer, Virgo, Scorpio, Pisces, Taurus, Capricorn

*Recommended Professions are: Childcare/Physical Therapist, Events Planners, Teachers, Managers, Nurses

The Cancer Personality

Cancer sign people are caring, trustworthy and loyal. They seek companionship, stability and security in their homes. Cancer people can appear casual, but they are deeply concerned about trusting others. Cancers are willing to lie to fix a relationship they love if it is in danger. If their moods are not balanced, they may lash out at other people without notice. Cancers enjoy being attentive to others and need to be noticed. The Crab symbol in their zodiac sign indicates that they are difficult to spot because of the protective shield they build. However, they love to help others and want to be understood.

* Strengths

* Weaknesses: Needy, Temperamental, Passive-Aggressive

Famous Cancer celebrities: Selena Gomez; Elon Musk; Ariana Grande, Post Malone Kristen Bell. Woody Harrelson

Leo

(July 23 to August 22).

* Motto: "I Will"

* Symbol:

* Element: Fire

* Sun, the ruling planet

* Birthstone: Peridot

* Key Personality Traits

* Compatible Signs: Leo, Sagittarius, Aries, Gemini, Libra, Aquarius

* Recommended Professions : Actors. Designers. Architects. Personal trainers. Teachers.

The Leo Personality

Leo's zodiac symbol, the Lion, is their personality trait. People of Leo are well-known for being brave, caring, and aggressive. But they will also be supportive of their family and friends. They are willing to fight for those who are poor, misunderstood, and less fortunate. Leos do not seek to be noticed or "center stage," but their natural instinct to lead often leads them to these situations. Although Leos appear strong on the outside they can be very sensitive to criticism and easily hurt. Leos can be insecure and cowardly and will try to conceal it by arrogance.

* Strengths: Heroic, Generous, Alluring, Protective

* Weaknesses

Notable Leo Celebrities include President Barrack Barack Obama, Jason Momoa and Jennifer Lopez. Charlize Thron, Neil Armstrong and Chris Hemsworth are some other notable examples.

Virgo

(August 23-September 22, 2008)

* Motto: "I Analyze"

* Symbol:

* Element: Earth

* Mercury is the Ruling Planet

* Sapphire is the Sapphire Birthstone

* Key personality traits: Competent, Perfectionists, Meek, Reserved

* Compatible Signs: Virgo and Capricorn, Taurus & Cancer, Scorpio

* Recommendations for Professions: Manager, Coach, Accountant, Analyst or Manager

The Virgo Personality

Virgo sign-born people are compassionate and supportive and love to organize the smallest details. It can be frustrating for them to be perfectionists and to not see the bigger picture. The Virgo symbol is the Maiden (sometimes known as the Virgin). She has the attributes of a provider and organizer. Her traits also include servant-like characteristics that are evident when she is surrounded with her loved ones. Virgos are a deep thinker and will do anything to make their lives better. They are honest and open-minded friends who will give constructive criticism, even if they don't have the best intentions. They are extremely attentive to their appearance and care about what other people think. They are quick to respond to threats or attacks and will not hesitate in expressing their anger. Virgos love giving and receiving love, and are happy to spend time with their family and close friends. They can be seen as being intrusive and nosy if they feel the need to ask questions. Virgos love to take on a challenge and thrive when they are in a supportive, mutually beneficial environment.

* Strengths

* Weaknesses: Perfectionist, Critical, Obsessive

Notable Virgo Celebrities - Pippa Middleton and Blake Lively, Beyonce, Blake Lively, Keanu Reeds, Salma Haek, Stephen King

Libra

(September 23 – October 22)

* Motto: "I Balance"

* Symbol:

* Element: Air

* Ruling Planet Venus

* Birthstone - Opal

* Key personality traits: Tactful and Discreet; Uncertain; Strong-minded

* Compatible Signs: Libra, Sagittarius, Aquarius, Leo, Gemini, Aries

* Recommended Professions : Stylists. Lawyers. Counselors. Graphic designers.

The Libra Personality

Libra is represented in the zodiac symbol The Scales. This symbol reflects the characteristic characteristics of Libra sign: A dreamer and a communicator. Librans are able to spend their time learning to understand themselves and to seek out solutions.

It is important to strike a healthy balance in love, career, and health. They are compassionate and care about the well-being of others. These people are very diplomatic and will help anyone in need. It can sometimes be hard to trust them. They are very good at avoiding conflict but if they have anger or frustrations buried deep, any small event can trigger them. Because they focus most of their attention on others, they sometimes neglect themselves, which can result in passive-aggressiveness; hence, their never-ending search for a healthy life balance.

* Strengths

* Weaknesses: Deceitful, Trusting, Materialistic

Notable Libra Celebrities Kim Kardashian & Will Smith, Avril lavigne, ZacEfron, Brie Hanson, 21 Savage

Scorpio

(October 23 – November 21).

* Motto: "I Desire"

* Symbol:

* Element: Water

* Pluto is the ruling planet

* Birthstone: Topaz

* Key personality traits: Passionate, powerful, focused, charming, charismatic

* Compatible Signs: Scorpio, Taurus, Virgo, Capricorn, Cancer, Pisces

* Recommended Professions : Marketer, Engineer, Pharmacist or Physician, Financial Advisor

The Scorpio Personality

Scorpio falls under this zodiac symbol: Scorpion. Scorpion-like traits include careful observation and quick strike. Scorpions will not hesitate to confront and approach anyone they find dangerous or dishonest. They don't share their emotions very often, but they will probe and dig to uncover the truth. They are very intuitive and have the ability to read others. Scorpio is a control freak and loves to analyze details and take control. Scorpio people have a vivid imagination. They can become jealous or suspicious if they get too excited. Scorpions love their family and will defend them. But, forgiving and forgetting is not something Scorpio people often think about. They will be vengeful if they have been wronged or betrayed.

* Strengths: Zealous, Ambitious, Passionate, Surrendering

* Weaknesses: Spiteful, Possessive, Critical, Suspicious

Notable Scorpio Celebrities

Sagittarius

(November 22 to December 21).

* Motto: "I See"

* Symbol:

* Element: Fire

* Jupiter, the Ruling Planet

* Birthstone: Turquoise

* Key Personality Traits

* Compatible Signs: Sagittarius, Libra, Aquarius, Aries, Leo

* Recommended Professions

The Sagittarius Persona

Sagittarius people are naturally lucky and can easily find new opportunities. Sagittarius is represented by the Centaur (or Archer) zodiac symbol. It combines human and animal traits. Archer traits are being straight-forward in their actions and words, with little concern for the impact they have on others. Sagittarius' personality is open-minded and seeks understanding. They are happy to help others, have a positive outlook and can inspire others. They are typically easy-going and easy going, but if they feel overwhelmed, insecure or wrongly charged, they will get violent. They can easily become overwhelmed by details and lose track of the important things. While they might make friends with many people along their adventures, they are careful to keep their family ties close to home and give themselves ample time for the most crucial relationships.

* Strengths

* Weaknesses

Notable Celebrities: Frank Sinatra, Taylor Swift, Mark Ruffalo, Scarlett Johansson, Jon Stewart, Tina Turner

Capricorn

(December 22-January 19, 2018)

* Motto: "I Use"

* Symbol:

* Element: Earth

* Saturn: The Ruling Planet

* Garnet is the birthstone

* Key personality traits: Reliable, persistent, ambitious, ambitious, influential

* Compatible Signs: Capricorn, Virgo, Scorpio, Pisces, Taurus, Cancer

* Recommended Professions : Human Resources, Computer Programmer. Electrician. Nursing. Accountant.

The Capricorn Personality

Capricorns, like the Sea Goat zodiac sign, are known for being confident and strong-willed. Capricorns have a strong social side and are willing to argue to prove their points. They are calm and well-organized. Capricorns don't trust people easily, so it takes patience. Their tendency to isolate from others can cause them to internalize emotions, which can make them depressed, self critical, and very pessimistic. They love spending time with the people they trust and they feel more fulfilled when they are able to form relationships. If they find someone manipulative or aggressive they will quickly and readily reject them.

* Strengths

* Weaknesses: Rigid, Pessimistic, Skeptical

Notable Celebrities Michelle Obama. Aaliyah. Jeff Bezos. Betty White. Muhammad Ali. Dolly Parton. Elvis Presley.

Aquarius

(January 20 to February 18)

* Motto: "I Know"

* Symbol:

* Element: Air

* Uranus, the Ruling Planet

* Birthstone: Amethyst

* Key Personality Traits

* Compatible Signs: Aquarius, Gemini, Libra, Sagittarius, Aries

* Recommended Professions : Teacher, Political Activist Artist, Astrologer Scientist

Aquarius Personality

Aquarius sign is known for being curious, eccentric, and energetic. The Water Bearer zodiac sign represents this sign. Aquarius people are rebellious in spirit, highly motivated, and energy. They are willing and able to listen to other people and provide assistance when needed. They may seem odd or bizarre to others but enjoy the reaction of others. Because of their energy, they can get bored easily and will go out looking for something stimulating. These people are reliable and focused on building long-lasting relationships.

* Strengths: Friendly, Intelligent, Innovative, Philanthropic

* Weaknesses: Detached, Irresponsible, Rebellious, Forgetful

Notable Aquarius Celebrities Oprah Winfrey Michael Jordan Jennifer Aniston Ashton Kutcher Ellen DeGeneres Bob Marley

Pisces

(February 19-20, 2010)

* Motto: "I Believe"

* Symbol:

* Element: Water

* Neptune is the ruling planet

* Aquamarine is the Birthstone

* Key Personality Traits

* Compatible Signs: Pisces, Capricorn, Taurus, Cancer, Scorpio

* Recommended Professions

The Pisces Personality

Pisces's zodiac symbol is The Two Fish. It represents wisdom and gentleness. People born under this sign have a tendency to be creative, intuitive, and malleable. They seek harmony and are happy to be involved in charitable and community activities. Their desire to help others can make them lose their mind and lead them to become too interested in gossip and drama that is not appropriate for them. They are not good at making decisions because they don't want to disappoint others. They may be manipulated because they are sensitive to the needs of others. They lack the ability and discipline to set boundaries. This makes them vulnerable to manipulation. Pisces are trustworthy and loyal.

* Strengths

* Weaknesses: Co-dependent, Submissive, Naive

Celebrities in Pisces are: Steve Jobs (Steve Jobs), Sophie Turner (Steve Irwin), Drew Barrymore (Adam Levine), Rihanna (Rihanna).

Attracting Love through Astrology

Astrology offers valuable insight into how others and ourselves are influenced by common traits. You can use this tool to attract love or in other relationships. It is possible to draw someone into a romantic relationship by using certain aspects of each zodiac symbol.

There are many ways to lure the various Astrological Signs.

Aries: Aries enjoys engaging conversation that stimulates their minds. They are also open to people who show a healthy amount of confidence. This sign is always looking for a challenge. If you work hard, you will be considered the prize.

Taurus: When you are determined to win the Taurus' attention, do something nice or treat them to dinner at their favorite spot. They aren't attracted to flirtatious, sexy personalities. Instead they like to spend time together with someone who is smart and sensual. Tauruses appreciate patience and are not fond of being pressured. They will reciprocate your kindness once you have gained their trust.

Gemini: Geminis are open to being complimented about their intellectual and physical abilities. Geminis enjoy a lively debate and want a partner who is independent, self-confident, and independent. Geminis are attracted to style and good self-care. Most likely, this is evident by their physical appearance.

Cancer: Cancer attracts complexity and people who are both sweet and tough. They don't like games and are difficult to trust, so be open and honest in your conversations. Keep in touch with them, sharing a smile and your admiration. Although you may be the one who opens up first, it is likely that you will win their trust.

Leo: Leo is an individual who loves being noticed. Be sure to compliment them and give them lots of attention. Leos are strong and confident, and they also like people who share these traits. Do not play games with Leo. Instead, be straight-forward and honest. If you can make Leo giggle, you'll soon find your way to their heart.

Virgos: Virgos tend to be very organized and plan-oriented. They value control and prefer to be in control. They don't attract people who are intellectually and self-assured. As a observer, you can help them to see and appreciate their unique qualities. The same goes for their weaknesses. Use this to your advantage and show support. Virgo loves to be made laugh at by someone. Once you get their attention, pause long enough to persuade them to find out more about your personality. This keeps Virgo occupied and helps to keep him from becoming bored.

Libra: Libras love to be around people who are open-minded, spontaneous, and cooperative. They are attracted to attention. Talking about your hobbies and interests will be interpreted as flattery. Instead of asking them out on next week's date, try to get them to join you for a quick cup of coffee.

Scorpio: Scorpio doesn't want to be the first one to tell you they are interested. Take it slow and engage in lighthearted, fun activities. However, if they express their love for you, don't be afraid to say so unless it is a risk of making them feel rejected. You will see them move in the opposite way if they do. Scorpios will be interested in you if you show them that you are good listeners by recalling details they shared with your.

Sagittarius. As a natural dreamer and someone who often wears their emotions on their sleeves, almost all that is required to attract the attention of a Sagittarius are a detailed conversation about your goals. This will encourage them to stand beside you and help make your dreams come true. Your mutual support in helping them reach their goals is the only thing they want in return.

Capricorn: Capricorns are attracted to stability and good conversation. Capricorns tend to avoid shallow, aloof and irresponsible people. They are attracted to people that remind them of themselves. You'll be able to have an intelligent conversation with this person and make them feel comfortable.

Aquarius: Aquarius likes people who are clever, unconventional, and can start a conversation. Aquarius is very protective of one's privacy so it's best to avoid having too many physical contacts at first. If you're a good match, physical relations will eventually develop. The Aquarius is a person who values friendship and respects others. This person likes to be around people who are kind, intelligent, positive, optimistic, and well-versed.

Pisces - Pisces isn't interested in superficiality, which is crucial when trying to attract their attention or infatuation. Do something that is meaningful. Giving them a unique gift, writing a personalized note, or planning a date to make an impression. Pisces is a person who longs to be understood. Your actions will communicate this and you will gain their trust, respect, and companionship.

Astrology has many moving parts, as we've already discussed. You might be wondering, perhaps, how two people born in the exact same month or on the exact same day can have such different traits. These details will be covered in detail in the following chapters, which cover the 12 Houses as well as the Influence and Planets.

The relationship between signs, houses, or planets is sometimes called the How, What, and Where. For example, the signs of astrology are filled with characteristics and traits that are often found in people of certain signs. Thus it is "How" someone's energy is expressed. The "Where", which is based on relationships and people, represents the 12 houses that represent how attitudes and perceptions will play out. Finally, the "What" is about the planets. The placement of the planets and the house in which you live will affect your environment, experiences, and overall outlook. The planets are often compared to archetypal or spiritual energy. So think about your friends, family and neighbors as well as their interactions with you and other people.

Chapter 11: The 12 Houses of Astrology

Astrology is so fascinating once you get to know the workings and details of the 12 Houses. In short, the 12 Houses are a map of the past, present, future. Each house correlates with the planet of the birth date, time, location.

To make it more clear, the twelve signs of the zodiac are determined by the Earth rotating around the sun over the course a full year. While the twelve houses are determined by the Earth rotating 24 hours per day and the influence from the planets' movements and their movements,

It is easy to view the houses as "fields or experience" where the "energies," of the elements, planets and zodiacs manifest. Each person moves between the 12 houses every day because they are in a 24-hour rotation. They also change every 4 mins. It is important to know the exact time of birth when trying to understand the natal charts. These details explain why people born on different days and at different times can have drastically different personalities.

There are many symbolic connections to the 12 Houses. Each House represents a stage of development. For example, the first house is about the beginning of your life.

Understanding the 4 Angular Houses

There are four houses that can be described as "action or angulous" within each of the 12 Houses. They include Houses 1, 4, 7, 10, and 10. These houses focus on relationships and career. These angular houses can be considered the four main entrances to astrology.

These houses correspond with the zodiacs Capricorn Libra Cancer Aries. You can deal with whatever life throws at you by determining the signs and orientation points for your house and the planets.

* The First House corresponds directly with your ascendant sign. It will enhance certain

traits. It is responsible for your outward appearance, your approach, and mannerisms.

* The Fourth House lies exactly opposite the Tenth House. It will govern your roots and influence your early life experiences.

* The Seventh House pairs well with the First House as well as the descendant angle. It manages both your friends and enemies.

* The Tenth House governs career, professional and personal achievements as well as the sense of purpose and life's direction. It is found at the highest point of chart and corresponds to Midheaven angle.

The horizontal lines and the meridian are what create the angles in the chart. East/West and North/South.

The four angular house, also known as the cardinal, have the greatest influence. You can also find important components in the angles created by the cusps.

The Signs of the Four Angles of the Natal Chart

* The eastern horizon is on the left. This is the location of the "Ascendant", also known as the AC Angle. Your Ascendant sign can determine how others see you and your family.

* The DC Angle (or "Descendant") is located at west horizon to the right. The sign represents you and your partner's characteristics.

* The highest point is the "Midheaven" (or MC Angle). Your legacy will be enhanced and your career choices improved by knowing your midheaven sign.

* The MC is opposite the "Imum Coeli" or IC. Latin Imum Coeli can be translated as "bottom of sky", which could also translate to foundation. The zodiac sign at this angle will indicate your preferences for home and surroundings.

Knowing how the houses relate to you personally is an important part of understanding your "Ascendant" (or "Descendant") axis.

It is important to know the Ascendant sign and the Descendant sign in order to interpret your birth chart. Your Ascendant sign plays a significant role in how others relate to you. This sign, also called the rising sign, is located on either the Eastern or far left sides of your chart.

The Descendant sign corresponds to the sign that is exactly opposite. It is located on the western sky when you were born. This axis represents your levels of cooperation and commitment, mindfulness of others, and relationships. The Descendant sign of your birth chart will have a significant impact on how you deal with these aspects.

Midheaven: It is the most important aspect of your career and your reputation. The Imum Coeli also represents the basic needs of security, family and home, as well self-destructive tendencies.

The 12 Houses - Explained

The "House of Self", the 1st House, is the symbol of all the firsts of life. It also has an impact on how you were born and how it influenced others.

* Astrology Sign: Aries

* Mars as a Natural Ruling Planet

* Representations from the 1st Haus: Initial impressions, new start, self-awareness. Attitude and views about life. The planets that are based on where you were born will have an impact on your character and the way others react to you.

The 2nd House is known as the "House of Possessions" and refers to your material possessions, financial situation, and attitude about these things.

* Astrology Sign Taurus

* Ruling Planet Venus

* Representations from the 2nd Haus: Your daily habits, work ethic, career status and the way that you prioritize your belongings.

The "House of Communications", which is located in the 3rd House, determines the foundation of your communication skills related to community, educational, and interpersonal influences.

* Astrology Sign: Gemini

* Mercury is the Ruling Planet

* 3rd House Representations: Communication and reasoning skills, intellect and mode of thinking.

The "House of Home and Family", The fourth House: The 4th House stands for the "foundation" of your family, including your home and security.

* Astrology Sign: Cancer

* Moon, the ruling planet

* Representations from the 4th House: home and family dynamics, roots, emotions.

The "House of Creativity", which is located in the 5th House, promotes the playful, joyful, and spirit-filled part of your life. It's where you'll find personal expression as well as all the things that are fulfilling and inspiring.

* Astrology Sign Leo

* Sun, the ruling planet

* Representations from the 5th House: Romantic relationships. Creativity, playfulness, fun, and self-expression.

The "House of Service and Health", the 6th House, is where many of the responsibilities of life are managed and ultimately control your daily life. The facets include your routines, schedules as well as personal and professional health and fitness.

* Astrology Sign: Virgo

* Mercury, the Ruling planet

* Representations for the 6th Haus: Personal sense and quality of use, service and help offered, work ethic.

The 7th House (House of Marriage and Partnerships): This House governs personal and professional relationships. It also governs our attitude to these relationships and our handling of competition. It is the main focus of our relationships with other people that motivates us in securing contracts, committing to marriage and making official dealings with them.

* Astrology Sign: Libra

* Ruling Planet Venus

* 7th House Representatives: Social demeanor, equality, sharing of life, relationships.

The 8th House, also known as "House of Death and Regeneration", is also called "house of sex and tax". It is the house where one holds onto their limitations, bad attitudes, secrets and fears. The 8th House, in the end, is a house of transformation, and hence its association to regeneration. Instead of looking at it for the undesirable aspects of life it shelters, look at the 8th House in terms that it is capable to transform. No matter what it has held you back, take control of your past and begin to live the life you deserve.

* Astrology Sign: Scorpio

* Pluto, the ruling planet

* 8th House representations: Intimacy and bonds with others; sharing of resources; dealing with obligations; trust. How these details affect personal transformation.

The 9th House, also known as "House of Mental Exploration", is the place to explore the higher mind and look beyond our material limitations. This house can help us grow and overcome our fears.

* Astrology Sign: Sagittarius

* Jupiter, the Ruling Planet

* Representations the 9th House. The 9th House has a focus upon discovery, religion, or philosophy. This influences one's outlook and values. It also refers to wealth, wisdom and the desire for greater learning.

The 10th House represents the "House of Career". It is situated at the highest point of the Birth Chart and is considered the highlight of personal life and your success. This house is a place where courage and ambition are celebrated, as well as professional goals or achievements.

* Astrology Sign Capricorn

* Saturn: The Ruling Planet

* Representations to the 10th House Public persona You will see the fruits of your hard work and best achievements, and you will be acknowledged.

The "House of Hope and Wishes/ Friendships", 11th House: This house encourages you to put your focus on the outer world. It can be about relationships or putting in effort for the greater good. It is here that one finds their spirituality.

* Astrology Sign Aquarius

* Uranus, the Ruling Planet

* Representations for the 11th Haus: Friends, wants, social awareness, and group participation. The 11th House houses our ability to use our talents and create a better future for all.

The 12th House (House of Self-Undoing): This 12th House is also the last house. Therefore, the name selfundoing. The 12th House is the "House of Self-Undoing": All of life's experiences have been absorbed. This house allows us to stop focusing on our individuality and instead just want to be. This is also called the "unseen domain", and it can be used to refer to isolation from the world in search of deeper meanings, or work with people who need extra care and compassion.

* Astrology Sign - Pisces

* Neptune is the ruling planet

* Representations from the 12th House, Surrender (disability), karma (and restitution).

It is sensible to consider the houses as places for enlightenment. If you can understand the relationship of the houses to the planets based upon the date, time, and place of birth, it is much easier to analyze personality traits and temperaments as well how an individual processes information.

The 12 houses signify different situations and areas in life. The planets, on the other hand, represent the diverse needs, wants and drives that people have. Astrology plays an important role. The moon and sun are not planets. However, they are listed here for convenience.

There are three main categories for the astrological ten planets.

* Personal planets: The Moon and Sun, Venus, Mercury and Mars

* Collective Planets Pluto, Uranus, Neptune

* Social Planets, Jupiter and Saturn. These two planets are considered to be the transitional ones

The pace at which planets traverse the zodiac chart varies. However, the speed of the personal planets is slightly faster. For example, Mars takes 40+ days to travel between the zodiac sign while the Moon only moves between them once every few days. The collective planets travel much faster, sometimes taking months or even years.

Astrology can refer to the state of a planet as "retrograde" (or "stationary") depending on whether it is in retrograde or stationary. Retrograde refers when a planet appears as if it is going backwards but is actually moving slower. If a retrograde planet is on your natal charts, then the emotions that correspond with it will be more intense. Only the 8 planets are retrograde; not the sun and the moon.

Below are descriptions about the planets, and how their archetypal energys impact on your life.

Sun: Your interests, preferences, strength and motivational drive are all affected by the Sun. It is related to your father, Masculine energy.

* Journeys Between Signs: Each month

* Symbol:

* Psychology: "I Am"

* Rules: Leo

When it comes to how you interact in your world with other people, the Sun is the most significant planet. It is the core of what governs your individuality.

Moon: Moon has a direct effect on your moods and emotions. It affects your ability to react, communicate, and openly share with others. It impacts your security or insecurity, routines, comforts and instincts, as well. It is associated with the feminine or nurturing energies (e.g., your home, family members and mother)

* Journeys Between Signs: 2 - 3 days

* Symbol:

* Psychology: "I Feel"

* Rules: cancer

Moon ruler planets can make you more attuned to your emotions and inner instincts.

Mercury: Mercury influences your communication and brain. This affects how you learn, problem solve and communicate. Mercury's retrograde position at your birth would mean that you are more intuitive and take time to think before you speak. Being born when Mercury was stationary, however, would make you an extremely big thinker and someone who loves to talk.

* Journeys Between Signs: 3 - 4 weeks

* Symbol:

* Psychology: "I Think"

* Rules: Gemini & Virgo

Mercury is the planet that rules your expression, processing, and perception. Mercury-ruled people tend to be intelligent and gifted, but also sarcastic. They are quick-witted and analytical. The "personal", fast-moving planet that is also a fleeting one determines the level of tactility, tone and bluntness in communicating with others.

Venus: Venus is another one of the fast-moving inner bodies. This means that the inner planets have a more significant impact on everyday life. It exhibits many feminine characteristics such as beauty, harmony and attraction.

* Journeys Between Signs: 4 - 5 weeks

* Symbol:

* Psychology: "I Love"

* Rules for Libra and Taurus

Venus is the ruler of Libra and Taurus. It is worth noting the similarities between these zodiac signs. Libra enjoys elegance, sophistication and lavishness. Taurus is drawn to material and indulgent pleasures. Venus is named after a goddess. It influences one's perception, reactions, opinions, and views on love, beauty charisma, grace, and grace.

Mars: Mars rules action, aggression. Mars is small compared to other planets. However, its fiery red color is a symbol of intensity and strength. Mars was named after the Roman God of War. It represents survival instincts and all human basic instincts.

* Journeys Between Signs: 6 - 7 weeks

* Symbol:

* Psychology: "I Act"

* Rules Aries

It is not surprising that Mars, the ruler of Aries knows how to get things done. Mars is the ruler of Aries' leadership traits of passion, self expression, and confidence. Mars' energy can be a motivator but if it's not properly harnessed, it can cause impulsive, kneejerk reactions. This can make it difficult for people to succeed. When used correctly, however, it can be a powerful motivator that can help you overcome difficulties and achieve your goals.

Jupiter: Jupiter is responsible to optimistic attitudes, empathy and a desire of growth. Jupiter also provides guidance for those who are on a journey to find happiness and purpose. Jupiter is often seen as a symbol that represents wealth, influence, abundance and power.

* Journeys Between Signs: 12 -13 months

* Symbol:

* Psychology: "I Grow"

* Rules: Sagittarius

Jupiter rules Sagittarius. This planet is known for its influence on attitude, confidence and tolerance. It can impact self-confidence, opinions and personal expression. Jupiter-ruled people are known for being passionate knowledge seekers and observing others with keen interest. They work tirelessly to become the best version of their selves. Jupiter-ruled individuals are also known to be philanthropists, philosophers, and have a tendency see the best of others.

Saturn: Saturn controls the limits of life, including fear, challenges, boundaries and responsibilities. This planet plays an important role in financial stability and career. If Saturn is in a stationary position at birth, people are more focused on their goals and self-discipline. Contrarily, when Saturn is retrograde at birth people are accountable for their failures and successes.

* Journeys Between Signs: 2-3 years

* Symbol:

* Psychology: "I Achieve"

* Rules: Capricorn

Saturn has a profound effect on the zodiac personality. It prompts self-assessment.

Saturn influences how you manage fear, deal with setbacks, fears, and other stressors. Saturn can be viewed as a reality check that is depressing, but it can also help you overcome difficulties and increase self-esteem and trust in your abilities.

Uranus - Uranus is the planet which inspires transformation and creativity. It is responsible to manage those tendencies to rebel and to feel more spontaneous. Uranus can be credited for those times when you have an epiphany or "aha!" moment.

* Journeys between signs: 7 years

* Symbol:

* Psychology: "I Evolve"

* Rules: Aquarius

Aquarius is ruled over by Uranus and people born there are outgoing, unpredictable, and adventurous. Uranus helps us decide who we are as individuals and how we wish to impact the world.

www.ingramcontent.com/pod-product-compliance
Lightning Source LLC
Chambersburg PA
CBHW071332120626
46546CB00002B/531